ESTRELLAS:
MOMENTS OF ILLUMINATION
ALONG EL CAMINO DE SANTIAGO

ESTRELLAS:
Moments of Illumination Along
El Camino de Santiago

A memoir

by

SUZANNE MAGGIO

Adelaide Books
New York / Lisbon
2021

ESTRELLAS:
Moments of Illumination Along *El Camino de Santiago*
A memoir
By Suzanne Maggio

Published by Adelaide Books, New York / Lisbon
adelaidebooks.org

Editor-in-Chief
Stevan V. Nikolic

For any information, please address Adelaide Books
at info@adelaidebooks.org
or write to:
Adelaide Books
244 Fifth Ave. Suite D27
New York, NY, 10001

ISBN: 978-1-956635-14-0
Printed in the United States of America

To my Camino family -
Thank you for sharing your light with me.
And to Bob, Tucker and Dylan -
the brightest stars in my sky.

Contents

"All men have stars, but they are not the same things for different people. For some, who are travelers, the stars are guides. For others they are no more than little lights in the sky. For others, who are scholars, they are problems... But all these stars are silent. You-You alone will have stars as no one else has them... In one of the stars I shall be living. In one of them I shall be laughing. And so it will be as if all the stars will be laughing when you look at the sky at night. You, only you, will have stars that can laugh! And when your sorrow is comforted (time soothes all sorrows) you will be content that you have known me... You will always be my friend. You will want to laugh with me. And you will sometimes open your window, so, for that pleasure... It will be as if, in place of the stars, I had given you a great number of little bells that knew how to laugh."

—The Little Prince, Antoine de Saint-Exupéry

A note...

The word *estrellas (pronounced ehs-treh-yahs)* means *stars* in Spanish. Because this story takes place in Spain, I use Spanish words common on the Camino throughout the book and provide translation whenever possible.

I kept a journal as I walked. It was a place for me to jot down impressions and observations, first thoughts and questions. I have included excerpts like this one interspersed in the pages that follow, particularly when the action of the story covers several days. While they are brief, I hope they give you a sense of what I was seeing and thinking as I walked along.

My entry on that first day began like this:

Day 0 - St-Jean-Pied-de-Port

I took the early morning walk to the Sants train station, through the familiar scenes of my old neighborhood. It felt great to be back in Barcelona, to revisit the sites I have missed since I was last here. Last night I had a wonderful visit with Elena. We ate tapas in the Barri Gòtic and caught up on the years since we'd last seen each other.

In Pamplona I stopped at a bank and grabbed a quick lunch before I took the bus to St-Jean. A lovely little town along a river. Beautiful cobblestone streets and stone buildings decked with window boxes. Tourist shops have Camino things - shells, walking sticks. The streets are filled with pilgrims.

I went to the information office to check in and got my first stamp. The second one from the gite. Wandered a bit, breathing in the sights and smells. Can't believe I'm really here. Feeling nervous and excited. Ready to go.

PROLOGUE

"Wherever you go, there you are."
—*Buddhist saying*

Despite evidence to the contrary, I do not think of myself as a particularly courageous soul. I am not content to bask in my accomplishments nor do I spend much time tooting my own horn. I wasn't raised that way. I was taught to downplay my successes. To steer clear of vanity. I was raised to be humble. So, as I sit down to write this, I hope you'll forgive me for saying something completely out of character, but I feel the need to tell you that 779 kilometers is a long way to walk - and I took every single step.

The bus pulled up to the curb in St-Jean-Pied-de-Port and I stepped off. The hiss of the opening door still rang in my ears. As I stood on the sidewalk, the sun warmed my skin. I watched the bus pull away and then took a look around, surveying my surroundings. The old walled town, with white-washed buildings and red tile rooves, brought to mind a Cezanne painting. Tourists clambered across an old stone bridge. The waters of the Nive River glistened in the afternoon light and the streets were abuzz with people.

On any given day, hundreds of pilgrims carrying backpacks come to this place in the French Pyrenees. Strangers who have traveled from all around the world, from Hong Kong and Germany, Sweden and Australia, India and South Korea. They flood the streets, purchasing scallop shells and sampling their first pilgrim meal before bunking down for the night. In the morning, before the sun sits high in the sky, they will begin their journey. They have come to walk the Camino de Santiago.

I don't remember the first time I heard about the Camino, this 779-kilometer (500 mile) pilgrimage across the north of Spain. Perhaps like me you've watched Emilio Estevez' poignant film *The Way*, the story of a man who travels to this small town on the French border to retrieve the ashes of his son who died while crossing the Pyrenees mountains. The father, played by Martin Sheen, decides to complete the journey his son began, to the sacred cathedral in Santiago where the bones of St. James the Apostle are believed to be buried. As he completes the journey his son could not, he sprinkles his ashes along The Way.

Many people have heard of pilgrimages to Jerusalem or Rome, but over the years the Camino de Santiago de Compostela, or *The Camino* for short, has become one of the most popular in its own right. The Camino has been traveled for more than a thousand years and some believe it even pre-dates Christian times. While the Camino Frances, the route that Martin Sheen takes in the movie, is considered the traditional Camino, there are actually several routes to Santiago, through Spain and Portugal. In fact, it may have been the two northern routes, the Camino del Norte and the Camino Primitivo, that King Alfonso ll himself took in the 9th century. The route I walked, the modern version of the Camino Frances, was fashioned in the 1980s by a priest, Father Elias Valiña from the Galician village of O Cebreiro, who marked the ancient route with directional indicators of blue and yellow shells.

As I wandered along, it was difficult not to imagine the hundreds of thousands who had walked these same roads. They were are all around me. In the air I breathed and the dust that stuck to my shoes. In the warm embrace of the sun or the cool kiss of an afternoon shower. I would feel their presence rustling in the fields of wheat and hear their voices in the quiet stillness of a morning on the meseta. I would try to imagine, as I passed a flock of long haired sheep, a weary shepherd stumbling upon the bones of James, son of Zebedee and brother of John the Evangelist. The bones, buried deep in his field, had been there for more than 800 years. What must he have thought when he found them? Did he recognize the importance of his discovery? And then, when King Alfonso ll ordered the bones buried in a small chapel while he waited for a large cathedral to be built in Santiago, could he have ever imagined the numbers of visitors who would make the journey to this holy place?

A Christian pilgrimage, The Camino is often walked as a spiritual quest; less of a hike and more a transformative journey. For many who walk, their intention is clear, their purpose sure. But not everyone who walks does so with religious intent. I'd been raised Catholic and certainly was no stranger to the notion of a religious journey, but like many of the people I met, I was not conscious of any such motivation for walking. Spiritual transformation was far from my mind on the morning of May 31, 2019, when I set off on my journey.

I'd come for an adventure, one that I imagined would tax my physical capabilities and push me to explore my resolve. In the days and months leading up to my departure, I'd set about preparing as one does for a trip. I bought supplies, made the necessary arrangements and packed my bag. I visualized that first climb through the Pyrenees, the most difficult of the whole Camino. I imagined the sense of accomplishment, the triumph of those final steps into Santiago.

What I knew about the Camino I'd learned by reading books and scouring websites. I soaked up information like a dry sponge. Filled with answers to the questions I had, they would provide me with details and advice that would assist me on my way.

I learned that, walked in stages, the entire journey took a month or more to complete. Travelers, known as pilgrims, followed a series of shell markers and yellow arrows, crossing through cities and towns, over rocky mountain paths and through lush green vineyards, across sun baked fields and rain-soaked hills. While many walked the full route, others completed only a part of it. The most common section was the final 100 kilometers, from Saria to Santiago de Compostela, and while most people made the journey on foot, it was possible to cycle as well.

Pilgrims carry a small passport called a *credencial* and collect ink stamps from various places to mark their progress. You must have two stamps for each day of walking, so I collected stamps wherever I could; at cafes and albergues, churches, monasteries and museums. At the end of the journey, upon arrival in the town of Santiago, one presents their credencial to the pilgrim office as evidence of completion. It is then that you receive your *compostela*, the Certificate of Achievement.

The days are long. You rise early in the morning, sometimes before the sun, and walk until mid to late afternoon, stopping for breakfast and lunch along the way. Food along the Camino is plentiful. There are cafes and restaurants, small grocery stores and outdoor markets. The meals are simple. *Tortilla*, a Spanish omelet of sorts made with egg, potato and onion, and *bocadillos*, ham and cheese sandwiches on crusty bread, are daily indulgences, as is *café con leche* (coffee with steamed milk), *cerveza* (beer) and *vino* (wine). In the evenings many *albergues* (simple shared lodgings) offer pilgrim meals served communal style for a few euro.

The Camino is an exercise in simplicity. Most pilgrims carry their belongings in a pack on their back, mindful to take only what they will need. Some send their bags from town to town, opting to walk without the extra weight. Despite the myriad of advice and recommendations, there is no correct way to walk the Camino. Those who walk are fond of reciting the familiar refrain, "*You walk your own Camino.*" What that is, is left for you to determine. Discovery is part of the journey.

At night you fall into bed, equal parts exhausted and exhilarated, your feet throbbing from the long day of walking. Sleeping accommodations are varied. Most traditional are the albergues; simple, dormitory style rooms with bunk beds and shared bathrooms. But there are also hotels and hostals (simple, family-run accommodations which tend to be slightly cheaper than hotels) for those nights when the creature comforts of a private room, a comfortable bed and a relaxed, hot shower will do. Most nights I was in bed before the sun went down.

I walked between 20 and 30 kilometers a day (12 – 18 miles). Some days were shorter, others longer. One kilometer is about .6 miles, something you have to get used to when you travel outside the United States. I followed the recommended stages in my guidebook but there are a number of options as guidebooks vary. Still others find their own pace. Either way it's a lot of walking. Like many people who walk, I spent months in training, hiking with friends. But weekend jaunts are no substitution for life on the Camino. Although I thought I was prepared to walk the long distances, I found it entirely different walking day after day. The pace is yours to decide however. You don't have to put in the long miles I did.

But, as prepared as I thought I was when I stepped off that bus and made my way into town, I could never have predicted the journey I was about to embark on as I took those first few steps. Now, as I look back, I realize that the questions I had were the easy ones, the ones whose answers could be found within the pages of a guidebook or traveler's blog. What I did not know, was that harder questions awaited me. Questions I could not predict. Questions that could not be answered by others. Questions that had yet to reveal themselves to me.

The journey does not end in Santiago. One must return home after their pilgrimage and it is often in the days, weeks and months after that the questions emerge, when you try to make sense of what you've just experienced. When the feet heal and the pack has been emptied. When the pictures are sorted and the stories shared. It is in those moments that the journey comes back to you. When the sound of church bells or the smell of Scotch Broom leaves you with a sense of longing. And it is then that you begin to understand, because it is a kind of understanding that cannot be had in the present moment. An understanding that requires a looking back, as you begin to connect the dots and realize where you have been.

And then there are the people.

What does the word family mean to you? If you had asked me that question many years ago, my answer would have been simple. Family is the people I am related to by blood. That's the way things were in the tight knit, Italian American family that I grew up in. My family shared my name, my looks and my history and served as a mirror that reflected a familiarity, a sense of myself I could count on. Family was home. And home, as Robert Frost once wrote, "Is the place where, when you go there, they have to take you in."

But the Camino would challenge that understanding. In the days and weeks that followed I would begin to build a different kind of family filled with people whose experiences, expectations and beliefs were different than mine. A family of choice rather than blood, and, like my own family, I would come to depend on them.

In all families there are exits and entrances. Individuals come and go. Sons and daughters move away. They get married and have children. People we love die. The same would be true on the Camino. Not everyone walks the full route. Some who intend to, cannot continue. While you may share the entire journey with several, you may see others only once. Over the course of my walk I would say goodbye many times. I was not prepared for that. Goodbyes have always been hard for me.

But there were also hellos. Like my own family, ours would shrink and expand. As I spread my wings and stretched out, I would meet new people and the table would grow. New friends filled the spaces others left behind.

You will meet some of them in the pages that follow. In the days ahead we would laugh and cry, sing and dance and share an experience that would change us in ways we could not yet imagine. Although we came from all the corners of the world with histories we did not share, we would find connection on a journey that, like a family, would bind us together long after we returned home.

In its simplest form, the Camino is a walk, a journey from one point to another. But as is true with all journeys, it has the potential to be so much more. Buried inside the wrapping of the Camino is an invitation to pay attention to the things we so often take for granted. To walk is to slow down. In the deliberate pace, in the kilometers of quiet, there is an opportunity to settle deep into the experience. To be curious. To stand in wonder.

This opportunity to reflect is perhaps the greatest gift of the Camino. It is a journey that can lead you to a place that will stay with you long after you finish walking. But one does not need to travel far away from home to be able to journey inward. It can be done wherever we are.

As you travel along with me on my journey, I invite you to take the opportunity to explore the spaces around you. Notice the way the sunshine peeks through the leaves of the dogwood tree. Listen to the gentle whirr of the wings of the humming-bird. Smell the salt in the sea air. Use your senses. Pay attention to the things that we are often too busy to see. To hear. To smell. Let them take you inward. See where the path leads you.

Buen Camino.

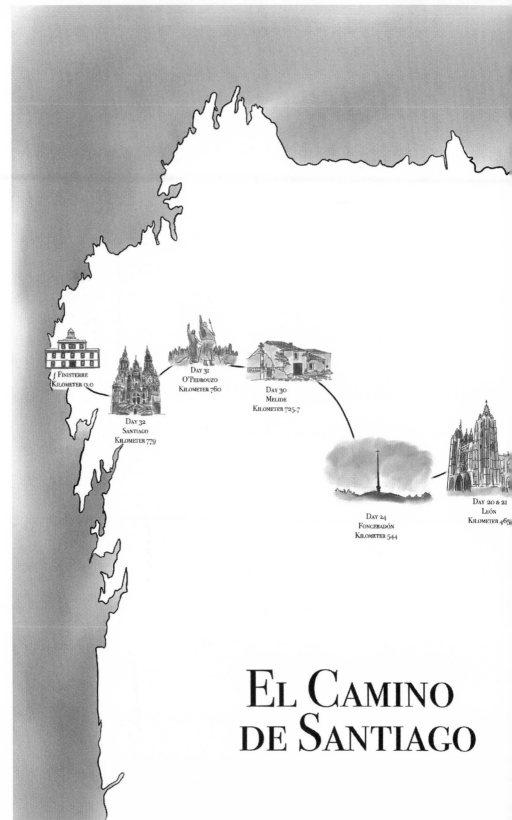

FINISTERRE
KILOMETER 0.0

DAY 31
O'PEDROUZO
KILOMETER 760

DAY 30
MELIDE
KILOMETER 725.7

DAY 32
SANTIAGO
KILOMETER 779

DAY 24
FONCEBADÓN
KILOMETER 544

DAY 20 & 21
LEÓN
KILOMETER 465

EL CAMINO
DE SANTIAGO

DAY 1
ST-JEAN-PIED-DE-PORT
KILOMETER 0.0

DAY 2
RONCESVALLES
KILOMETER 24.7

DAY 3
ZUBIRI
KILOMETER 47

DAY 4
PAMPLONA
KILOMETER 68.1

DAY 5
ESTELLA
KILOMETER 113.7

DAY 8
LOGROÑO
KILOMETER 163

DAY 16
ÓN DE LOS CONDES
LOMETER 370.7

DAY 9 & 10
NÁJERA TO BELORADO
KILOMETER 192.6

DAY 14
HONTANAS, KILOMETER
317.7

DAY 1
ST-JEAN-PIED-DE-PORT
KILOMETER 0.0

CHAPTER 1

Lean In

I am here.

The alarm went off before the sun rose in Barcelona that morning. I dressed quickly, brushed my teeth and stuffed my nightshirt into an outside pocket of my backpack before lumbering down the hotel stairs and out onto the sleepy street in the Eixample district. I knew it well. Just seven years before when I taught in a study abroad program, I'd lived in this neighborhood. The tree lined streets were empty and the neighborhood quiet but for the distant clatter of glass bottles being dumped into the back of the garbage trucks. I straightened my pack, clipped the buckle across my waist and made my way to Sants station.

I took the 6 a.m. train to Pamplona, dozing on and off as the train rocked back and forth and rumbled along the tracks. In Pamplona I caught a bus to St-Jean-Pied-de-Port, a small village along the French border. By the time I arrived it was almost dinnertime, so I found my albergue, dropped off my bag and went out to find something to eat.

I am filled with a strange mix of exhilaration and exhaustion. My feet roll over the cobblestones as I wander along the main street. The air is pregnant with the smell of spices and freshly baked bread. I pause to read a pilgrim menu posted on the wall outside a restaurant. I repeat this again and again as I amble down the street, trying to muster up the will to take the next step, to go inside. Finally, after I do this three or four times I conjure up enough courage to poke my head in, trying to gauge the lay of the land.

I have never been comfortable eating alone in a restaurant. I am self-conscious. Afraid that I will be noticed. That I will stick out like a sore thumb. Meals have always meant so much to me. I'd grown up in a large Italian family. Gathering around the table, passing plates of antipasto, gnocchi ala Bolognese and piping hot bread, meals were so much more than sustenance. It was a celebration. Of love. Of connection and belonging. There was nothing that made me happier than a table full of the people I love. The air ripe with a harmonious symphony of smells and voices. The more the merrier. To eat alone was to be alone. A sort of moral failing. Surely no one would choose to eat alone.

Years before, when I'd taught in Barcelona for a semester, I could not bring myself to dine alone in a restaurant. Not even once. When I wasn't cooking in my own apartment or gathered with friends I ate on the run, grabbing a hot, foil-wrapped sandwich and a bottle of water from the Doner Kebab on the corner rather than a steaming pan of paella and a glass of fruit forward Crianza at the restaurant right below my apartment. It was silly really. I'd been brave enough to travel 6,000 miles away from home to teach in a foreign country, but I couldn't bring myself to sit alone at a table covered with a white tablecloth and a proper napkin. It was one of the few regrets I had from that extraordinary time.

I'd promised myself this time would be different. It had to be. I had a month ahead of me and the potential for a meal or more alone was likely. I'd come home from that earlier trip feeling disappointed. I'd let myself down. I wasn't going to make the same mistake again. Now, as I faced the familiar struggle, my stomach was in knots. There's a saying in social work, my chosen career of more than 30 years, 'lean in to the discomfort'. Do what is hard. What makes you uncomfortable. I took a deep breath, reached out, turned the doorknob and walked through the door.

Diners stood two and three deep against the bar that ran the length of the room. I followed the host as she wound her way through a sea of faces and then outside into the garden. She showed me to a small table set for two, along a tall wooden fence that enclosed the outdoor dining area. I sat facing inward, my back to the wall. She handed me a menu and then, as if to put a punctuation point on my solitude, cleared the extra place setting. I settled in and ordered a glass of wine, the first of many I would enjoy over the next 30 days.

The unmistakable scent of cigarette smoke wafted through the air. To the right of me a couple of young women puffed away on French cigarettes. Growing up in a house where both parents smoked, it was a smell I'd always hated. Fortunately for me the laws had changed in recent years. In the United States, smoking was no longer allowed in restaurants or in many public spaces for that matter. Still, the rules were different here.

I ordered my first pilgrim meal, a stewed chicken and potato dish that came with a carafe of white wine. While I waited for the food, I paged through my Camino guidebook and eavesdropped on the conversations going on around me. The couple in front of me was speaking English. They sounded like they might be American. "Hello," I said, "Where are you from?"

"Arizona," they answered in unison.

"My son lives in Arizona," I said. "I'm from California. Are you walking the Camino?"

"Yes," the woman said. "We begin tomorrow."

"So do I. I'm excited and a little nervous."

"Same. The first day is supposed to be the hardest," the man said. "It's all uphill."

I nodded in agreement. I'd been thinking about the first day's walk for a while now, a rise of over 1400 meters in elevation from St-Jean-Pied-de-Port where we were, across the Pyrenees mountains to Roncesvalles, the place where I would spend the first night. The stage was also known for unpredictable weather. "I suppose it's better at the beginning than at the end. When we're still fresh." I smiled.

They nodded. "Are you alone?"

"Yes. I just got here this afternoon."

"Us too," the woman said. "My name's Debbie. This is my husband, Pat."

"Nice to meet you both. My name is Suzanne."

We chatted for a few more minutes while I waited for my food. Debbie was an elementary school teacher. Pat a financial consultant. They struck me as roughly my age. Like me, their children were grown. Unlike me, they had grandchildren. They'd lived in the San Francisco Bay area and gone to college at Chico State, one of many colleges in the state system where I currently taught. Like me they'd spent the months leading up to their Camino hiking in preparation. They'd even walked to the bottom of the Grand Canyon. I hadn't done anything quite that strenuous, spending weekends hiking on the trails in local parks. In fact, the longest hike I'd managed was a 10 miler with a couple of girlfriends. I hoped I was prepared.

I felt a quick comfort with them, a way in which they seemed like old friends. I found them easy to talk to. And, having chosen to come alone, I was curious about their decision to walk together. Our conversation drifted off a few minutes later when the waitress came with my dinner. I smiled to myself. *See,* I thought as I turned my attention to eating, *That wasn't so hard, was it?*

Without a dinner partner I found myself people watching, wondering how many of the faces that surrounded me now I would see in the days ahead. Fortunately, by the time I started to tuck in, the smokers at the next table had left. The food was decent, if non-descript, and I was hungry. I cleaned my plate and then polished off the fruit crisp for dessert. As I got up to leave, I stopped to say goodbye to Debbie and Pat. "Have a good night," I said. "Maybe I'll see you along the way."

After dinner I wandered around town for a little while, past the spice shop and the chocolatier. I stepped inside the church and lit a candle in memory of my parents, the first of many I would light along the way. I was back at the albergue before the sun even set.

The room was small, with a couple of bunk beds built into the wall. When I checked in, I'd claimed the bottom bed closest to the door and despite the fact that it was still early, the lights were off and there was already someone asleep in the top bunk at the other end of the room. I lay out my sheet and down quilt and changed into my pajamas. I climbed into bed and pulled the cream colored curtain across the opening, sealing myself in like a caterpillar in a cocoon. I closed my eyes and took a few deep breaths in an effort to settle in. My heart and mind raced. The excitement was palpable. What would tomorrow bring? In the stillness I could hear the faintest sound of my room-mate's snoring, a sound I would grow accustomed to as the days wore on. I pulled up the quilt and tucked it in under my chin. Tomorrow my adventure would begin.

Yet several hours later, I was still awake. I tossed and turned, twisting myself up in the cotton sheet. Voices rang out from the street below and floorboards creaked as a handful of pilgrims made their way up the stairs. The bathroom door closed. I heard a rush of water as someone turned on the shower. Soon, the door to the room opened. The beam of a small flashlight illumi-nated the darkened space and then came the thud of a backpack hitting the bench that ran the length of the room. Through the slit in the curtain I could see a pair of long muscular legs, close enough to touch. My anonymous roommate unbuckled his belt and the pants he was wearing fell to the floor. I closed my eyes to give him privacy.

I'd read Cheryl Strayed's memoir a few years earlier, about her 1,100 mile hike along the Pacific Crest Trail. With each step she took I'd marveled at her courage, envied her spirit and felt awed by her adventure. I had a desire to do something sim-ilar. To embark on a journey that had the potential to be life changing. To stretch myself. To push my own limits. To have time alone to think. But what?

And then one afternoon in late October, the *what* became clear.

It was a beautiful fall day in Northern California, the place I'd lived for more than 30 years. The crisp morning air had been replaced by warm mid-day sunshine. The leaves of the sugar maples in the front yard fell gently in the breeze and now the lawn was littered with a palette of reds and yellows and chartreuse green. The air still held the scent of freshly picked grapes from the nearby vineyards. Inside, my husband sat in his chair watching football as he did most weekends at this time of year. This afternoon, the San Francisco 49ers were losing to the Seattle Seahawks.

I walked in from the kitchen, having just put a pot of marinara sauce on to simmer. "I want to walk the Camino de Santiago de Compostela," I said. The words shot out of my mouth before I could even fully realize their meaning.

"Have a good time," he said without taking his eyes off the television.

I looked at him. "I'm serious," I said.

"I know you are," he said, turning towards me. "Go for it."

The night before we'd watched the Martin Sheen film "The Way", about the 500-mile hike across the north of Spain and, like I had when I read Strayed's memoir, I felt that same tug of excitement, a desire to take a journey of my own. Over the years there had been so many things I said I wanted to do. Things that for one reason or another, remained undone. Now, as the seed of this new adventure began to swell inside me, I knew I wasn't willing to let this be one of them.

The last few years had been difficult ones. Ever since my mother's death from Alzheimer's disease three years earlier, I'd had this strong sense that time was running out. Although she was almost 80 when she died, she was just 60 when she'd first begun to struggle. In those first few years her memory lapses seemed harmless. A lost set of car keys. A forgotten appointment.

The everyday challenges of having too many things to keep track of and an inevitable sign that she was growing older. But over time it grew worse. She lost track of entire conversations. Activities she no longer remembered. Soon it felt like we were trapped in an endless loop of repetition. It was clear that something more serious was going on.

When she was 70 years old, my father was diagnosed with ALS, Amyotrophic Lateral Sclerosis. The diagnosis came just a month before my parent's 49th wedding anniversary and my father's 72nd birthday. It followed a year in which he'd struggled with weakness in his legs, stumbling when he walked. The progression was quick. Early stumbles led to walking with a cane. By the time we understood what was happening, he was confined to a wheelchair. And then, a month after we received the official diagnosis, he was dead. A massive heart attack saved him and us, from having to watch the ALS metastasize throughout his body.

My father's sudden death exacerbated my mother's struggles. My siblings and I moved her closer to family, trying to take care of her as best we could. It would be several more years before we would get the official diagnosis of Alzheimer's disease, but by then it would be too late. In the last few years of her life she could not walk. She did not speak. She barely ate. In the end she no longer recognized any of us. Nineteen years after those early first signs, the disease erased my mother altogether.

My parents' health crises served as a reminder that things could change in an instant. A remembrance that there are no guarantees. I was about to turn 60, my birthday in little over a month. Although I was healthy, I carried with me a worry that I could not ignore. My own memory was not what it used to be. A career social worker, I'd prided myself on remembering the complex case histories of my clients. In the past decade I'd been teaching at the local university. Sometimes, as I stood in front of my students, words vanished from my mind. "Early onset Alzheimer's," I'd joke, and while my students laughed, I tried to disguise my worry. Now, as I began to confront my own challenges, I wondered if my mother recognized what was happening to her. She'd never said. And although I tried to reassure myself that memory lapses were normal, what if this was the start of something more serious?

And when the muscles in my legs ached. When I stumbled while crossing the street or when my legs gave out on me at the gym, my mind went to that dark place, a place I did not let myself go very often. *"You're going to be fine,"* I told myself. *"You're healthy. You are not your parents."* I'd done everything I could to take care of myself. I exercised regularly. Drank in moderation and I didn't smoke. Sure, I could stand to lose a few pounds, but who couldn't? I was going to be fine. Still, as much as I tried to reassure myself, I understood the unpredictability of life. Now, as my 60th birthday approached, I was keenly aware of the passage of time. There were things I wanted to do. Dreams I'd put off while raising my children, building a career and most recently, caring for my mother.

I'd always loved to travel. I'd recently become an Italian citizen and I even had an Italian passport. Sometimes I fantasized about living abroad, about owning a small apartment in the center of Rome or on a hillside in Tuscany where my husband and I could spend the summer months. As much as I loved my home in California, there was something that happened to me when I was in Europe that was hard to explain. As I walked along the city streets, drank cappuccino in an outdoor café or wandered around a weekend market, I felt an aliveness I had not known before. Europe was a part of me. Perhaps one day, I told myself, we might even live there permanently.

Except for one thing. Our kids were here. Sure, they were grown. They had their own lives and lived far away from us and the place they'd grown up. But they were a part of me, something I couldn't leave behind. We visited whenever possible. I wanted to stay involved in their lives. The fantasy of a life in Europe would have to wait.

My mother's death left me with a myriad of feelings to sort through, experiences and memories I'd been unable to process while she was alive. I'd spent the better part of the previous two years writing a memoir about our relationship. It had been a painful process that forced me to examine truths about myself and my family I had not wanted to see. In the end though, it allowed me to heal the pain I'd carried long after her death and make peace with a relationship that I'd struggled to understand.

The completion and publication of that book felt like a turning point of sorts, as if I were standing on the precipice of something new, although what, I did not yet know. I was about to enter a new phase of my life, one I hoped, despite my nagging fears of what might be, would be filled with possibility. I felt an urge to mark the moment, to celebrate my upcoming birthday. I wanted to do something that would challenge me.

"Maybe you can get Lynn to go with you," my husband said that fall afternoon. Bob was not a walker. "That's what cars are for," he'd declared whenever I suggested we walk into town. I wish I had a dollar for each time we'd argued as he circled the grocery store parking lot in search of a space closer to the door. If I were to walk the Camino, I could be sure he would not be coming along.

Lynn was one of my oldest friends. We'd known each other for more than 30 years and she was my go-to person when it came to outdoor things. She was athletic, upbeat and always ready for a challenge. Lynn was extraordinarily outgoing, an extrovert on the grandest of scales. She made friends wherever she went because there was no one she wouldn't talk to.

It would be fun to go with a friend, and Lynn would be the perfect companion, but I knew that if I went with her, I'd let her take the lead on social interactions. No, I needed to go alone. To challenge myself and experience the uneasiness that traveling alone would offer. To push myself past what was comfortable. To lean into the things that were hard for me. Going alone would allow me the opportunity to grow and the clearer that became, the more I was unwilling to compromise.

I would leave as soon as the spring semester ended. I circled a date on the calendar at the end of May and the Camino became my goal. In the months it took to get ready, I read dozens of books and articles written by people who'd walked before. I researched the best gear to bring and the perfect time to go. Bob offered to buy me a backpack for Christmas, so in late November I went to REI, our local outdoor store, to get fitted for one. The aisles were full of gear, more than I had ever imagined. Moisture wicking shirts, quick dry underwear and $20 dollar pairs of socks. Did I want wool or synthetic? Hiking boots or shoes?

Because I would be carrying everything on my back, weight mattered. As I began to gather the things I would take with me, I started to ask myself three questions: What did I *need*? What did I *want*? And what *couldn't I live without*? I needed comfortable shoes. I picked out a pair of Keens, a half size too big to give my feet room to swell. I bought a cotton sleep sheet, an inflatable pillow and a down quilt that squeezed into a small drawstring sack. For clothing I bought two of everything. One to wear and one to wash. Two t-shirts, two shorts, two socks, underwear and sports bras. Although I'd read that most people slept in their clothes, that wasn't going to work for me. I packed a cotton nightgown to wear instead. A rain jacket and rain pants. A warm overshirt. A pair of long pants. A headlamp. A swiss army knife. An almost useless travel towel that I hated more and more every time I used it. A combination spoon and fork. A bag full of toiletries. A cell phone and a camera. A small fanny pack where I would keep my money, my passport, my bank card and one credit card. And then I bought a one-way ticket to Spain.

I stuffed my belongings into the pack and propped it on the scale. The guidebook recommended carrying no more than 10% of your body weight. The weight wasn't exact, but the pack came in somewhere between 16 and 18 pounds. With the water I would carry each day, it was a little heavier than I wanted, but I would have to live with it. This was one dream that could not wait.

Early that first morning, as I lay tucked in my bunk and before my alarm even went off, I heard the sound of packs being zipped shut as pilgrims readied themselves to head out for the day. I turned off the alarm and checked the time. It was 5:45 a.m. *Welcome to the Camino,* I thought to myself.

To my surprise there was a text from my husband. "Have a great walk today," it said. "We're so proud of you."

I smiled. "Thanks," I texted back. "Today's going to be a hard one, but I'm ready." I slid out of bed and got dressed. I splashed some cold water on my face, brushed my teeth and dragged my pack to the dining room.

The room was spacious, a long, rectangular space filled with family style tables and a comfortable couch. There were trays full of yoghurt, fresh fruit and hardboiled eggs on the counter. Bread for toast and an assortment of pastries too. At the far end of the room was a big picture window and a door that led out to a quaint garden, with a grassy area, picnic tables, Adirondack chairs and a handful of clothes lines.

I peered out the window. The white stone houses were blanketed in fog and the sun had not yet begun to cut through.

"Good morning."

I heard the gentle voice as I set my bag against the wall. I turned to find a gray-haired woman smiling at me. She sat with a group of 3 other women at a table right beside me.

I smiled. "Good morning," I said.

I poured myself a cup of coffee, grabbed a strawberry yoghurt and a banana and sat down beside her. "Mind if I join you?" I asked.

"Of course," she said. "Where are you from?"

"California," I said. "And you?" I thought I heard an accent.

"Ireland. We're Sisters of Charity," she answered. "Is this your first time?"

I nodded, puzzled. I would soon learn that many walked the Camino more than once and as it turned out, this was also true for the nuns. One had walked the Camino four times.

I smiled to myself. I'd always had an affinity for nuns. In fact, I'd been known to take a picture or two of them when I'd come across them in my travels. Penguin pictures, I called them, calling forth the nickname from the old Blues Brother's movie. I'd been taught in high school by the Sisters of the Immaculate Heart of Mary, the "Big Macs" as they were known. I'd met many more of them over the years, both as a Jesuit Volunteer and then early in my career when I worked as a social worker at a number of Catholic elementary schools. Although not all of my interactions with them had been easy, I had a fondness for these women who dedicated their lives to the service of others and I respected their commitment.

The sisters I'd had in high school wore a full habit from head to toe, but these sisters were dressed in regular clothes, making their profession unrecognizable to the outside world. "Are you going to Roncesvalles?" I asked.

"Oh no, dear. We'll be spending the night in Orisson." She smiled warmly. "That's plenty for one day. We're in no rush."

I found it strange that the sisters were only going that far. Orisson was only 7.7 kilometers away, just a little over 4.5 miles. In my guidebook, the first stage was to Roncesvalles, 24.7 kilometers (15.3 miles) away. According to what I'd read, the walk would take about 7 hours. With the early morning start, that would put me there by midday. If there's one thing for certain, it is that I'm a rule follower. If the guidebook said that Roncesvalles was the first stage, well then who was I to argue? It hadn't occurred to me that people might make their own schedule.

But now, as I look back, I am struck by the randomness of it all. How the choices I made, from the day I started, to the guidebook I chose, to the schedule I followed, affected everything that was to come. From the weather as I crossed the pass to the people I would meet, the choices I made would have life changing consequences.

I peeled open the top of my yoghurt and ate it quickly. I poured myself one more cup of coffee and then bade farewell to the nuns. I was anxious to get going. "Have a good walk," I said before I walked down to the lobby to ask the *hospitalero* (albergue host) to stamp my *credencial*.

I stepped out onto the cobbled stones of the Rue Citadelle. There was a blueish tint to the world as the sun began to rise. Shopkeepers opened their doors and the smell of fresh baked croissants permeated the brisk morning air. The streets were quiet but for a few pilgrims who milled about, sipping coffee and making final adjustments to their packs. I paused and breathed in the moment.

Unsure of which way to go, I began to walk up the hill towards the Citadelle. At the top of the crest I paused and looked around. I was alone. The streets around me were empty. Soon, a pilgrim emerged from a doorway a few feet away and walked *down* the hill, towards town. I laughed and followed him. Not even one day in and I'd already gone the wrong way. There was so much that I had to learn. Still, I was finally on my way.

DAY 2
RONCESVALLES
KILOMETER 24.7

CHAPTER 2

Things

I trudged down the stairs of the monastery at Roncesvalles the next morning. Despite walking more than two dozen kilometers the day before, my feet felt surprisingly good. The line to the small office stretched past the glass doors and halfway down the hallway. Henrik, one of the group of Dutch hospitaleros, waved good morning and walked towards me. I'd met him two days earlier in the bus station in Pamplona while I waited to board the bus to St-Jean-Pied-de-Port.

The train from Barcelona on Thursday morning got me into Pamplona by midday. Pamplona was one of the hubs for transportation to the Camino with a bus to St-Jean-Pied-de-Port that left several times a day. That afternoon I wandered out to the terminal, my backpack slung lazily over my right shoulder and lilting awkwardly to one side. I'd managed enough Spanish to buy my ticket, but that was as far as I got. The woman in the ticket booth spoke so quickly I'd missed the directions about where to wait for the bus. There were no signs in the terminal, so I wandered out to the bus bay hoping to gather more information there. It hadn't helped. There were a dozen or more unmarked empty spaces and just a few people milling about. I slid off my pack and leaned it up against the wall.

"Are you on your way to St-Jean?"

I turned to find a man standing a few feet away. He was solidly built with grey hair and a wide face and I recognized his Dutch accent. He seemed about3 my age, perhaps a little older. I'd never been very good at guessing.

"I am," I said, "Although I'm not sure where to wait."

"Here," he said, motioning to the bus bay in front of us. "My name is Henrik. I'm on my way to Roncesvalles. You will be there tomorrow." He explained to me that he was a hospitalero, one of a group of volunteers from Holland who would staff the large municipal albergue in the monastery over the next two weeks. "I've been volunteering for a few years," he continued. "I began the year after I walked my own Camino."

We stood together and talked for a while. Buses came and went and soon the crowd for the bus to St-Jean began to grow. Henrik was from a small village in Holland I had not heard of. I told him I'd been to visit his country when I was much younger, to Amsterdam and Lisse to see the tulips. "It's a beautiful country," I said. I noticed the way my voice slowed, the way

I enunciated my words and simplified my language to make it easier for him to understand.

I smiled at myself. My maternal grandfather was born in Italy, coming to the U.S. as a young man. While his English was strong, he still spoke with a heavy Italian accent. My father, who was born and raised in Brooklyn, New York, lapsed into broken English whenever he spoke with him. We teased him mercilessly about it. It was an automatic response, one he never seemed to be able to manage. "It helps him understand me better," he'd said. Evidently the apple didn't fall far from the tree.

As we spoke more folks began to trickle in and soon the bay was full of people carrying backpacks. Before too long the bus pulled in and a line began to form. "I will see you in Roncesvalles," Henrik said.

"I'll see you there." I picked up my pack and took a place in line.

"Would you like me to reserve you a bed?" he called as I began to walk away.

"Sure. Is that allowed?" Remember, I'm a rule follower if nothing else.

"Of course," he laughed and pulled a slip of paper from his pocket. "Give me your name. I'll make sure you get a good bed. I think the third floor is best."

After leaving St-Jean on Friday morning just as the sun was beginning to rise, I'd made it to Orisson, the place where the Irish sisters were planning to stay, by midmorning. The stop was a favorite of pilgrims after the long 8 kilometer climb, a place to have a glass of freshly squeezed orange juice and take in the mountain vistas from the large wooden deck. I dropped my bag at an empty table and joined the queue inside. By the time I returned, I'd been joined by Debbie and Pat, the couple I'd met the night before and a new couple, Jeanette and Tim, from

Adelaide, Australia. The two couples had walked together that morning. Jeanette was a perky blonde, with a broad smile and a sunny disposition. Her husband Tim was a slight man with dark hair and fair skin, quieter than his wife but with eyes that twinkled and an impish grin. Within minutes, we hit it off.

It felt good to take a break after the strenuous climb, but soon I was ready to carry on. There was still a long way to go and I wasn't sure how long it would take me to get to Roncesvalles.

I arrived at the monastery after seven and half hours of walking, my feet sore but my heart full. The pilgrim lodging had been remodeled in recent years. Gone was the old one room dormitory that was featured in the movie *The Way* and in its place, a modern facility with three floors. On the grounds were several restaurants, a hotel, cafe and of course, a beautiful church.

I fished out my *credencial* and lined up with the others to secure a bed. That's when I saw Henrik. I raised my arm to wave hello.

"You made it," he said. "How do you feel?"

"Exhausted. But the walk was incredible."

He smiled a knowing smile. "Give this to the woman at the front of the line," he said as he handed me a small slip of paper. "She will give you a bed on the third floor."

I climbed the stairs and entered a large room filled with rows of single beds. The third floor, I found out later, was different than the first two which held rows of bunk beds, a layout common in the larger municipal albergues. The third floor was filled with beds grouped two to a pod, each separated by a half wall. The beds were numbered and I set out to find bed #300, the one I'd been assigned when I checked in. It was the last one in a long row of twenty that ran along the west wall. The bed was conveniently located near the bathroom. *Lucky for me,*

I thought, *I wouldn't have far to go if I needed it in the middle of the night.* I slid off my pack, dropped it on the floor and sat down on the bed. Every bone and muscle in my body ached. I couldn't remember ever being so tired. It was all I could do to unzip my pack and spread the cotton sleep sheet out on top of the mattress. I lay down and closed my eyes.

It had been a glorious, albeit difficult first day. The incline began almost immediately. Eight kilometers straight up along a paved trail that cut through pastures filled with grazing white long-haired sheep. Soon thereafter the path turned to dirt. Rolling green hills and blue mountainous vistas stretched as far as the eye could see. A weathered statue of The Virgin Mary holding the baby Jesus looked down on the valley. Debbie, Pat and I found a seat below her. I pulled off my socks to let my feet breathe and lay back in the grass, the blades sticking to my sweat dampened skin.

I remembered Martin Sheen's iconic walk up over this mountain in the movie. The fog and bitter cold swirled around him, engulfing his every step. At a rock cropping he paused for a moment, unsure of which way to go, But although we had been warned about the tendency for the weather to change quickly as one crossed the pass, ours could not have been more different. The sun beat down on us. Beads of sweat dripped down my face and stung my eyes. At the crest of the mountain I stopped to catch my breath. Rock croppings and the twisted horns of grazing sheep dotted the emerald landscape. Layers of blue mountain silhouettes capped in snow rose in the distance. Miles of trail as far as the eye could see lay ahead.

Soon, as I lay on the bed, my mind full of the day's images, I began to hear voices. A steady stream of pilgrims began to claim the beds around me. Although I wanted nothing more than to just stay right where I was, I knew that if I didn't get up soon, I'd have to wait in line for a shower. I willed myself to sit up, bent over to pull off my socks and slipped on a pair of sandals. Digging into my pack I grabbed my soap, shampoo and clean clothes and shuffled into the bathroom.

It was all I could do to undress. I moved slowly, as if through quicksand. Every part of me ached. I turned on the shower and slowly eased my hand under the spray. *Thank god, I thought.* Hot water poured from the showerhead. My first shower in St-Jean had been a cold one.

In the basement was a laundromat staffed by the Dutch hospitaleros. For a few euro you could wash and dry your clothes in proper machines, but it seemed silly to pay money to wash the handful of things I had. I filled a basin with warm water and dipped my clothes in, scrubbing each piece with the bar of soap I'd just used to wash my body. After a thorough rinse, I found a space on the large web of clothesline strung just outside the door and hung the pieces to dry. It was an exercise I would repeat again and again in the next 30 days.

There was an hour before dinner. Two, before Mass was scheduled to begin. I walked down to the bar and found a group of pilgrims sitting at some outdoor café tables, just a few hundred yards from the monastery. Debbie and Pat were there, along with a few faces I recognized from the day's walk. I ordered a tinto de verano, a refreshing mixture of red wine and lemon - lime soda, and found an empty seat.

At Mass that evening, dozens of people filled the Iglesia de Santa Maria. I slid into the pew and settled into the spaciousness around me. The old cathedrals were always a favorite of mine. I loved the way the pillars climbed to the ceiling, like vines that search for the sunshine. The mesmerizing kaleidoscope of colors in the rose windows of the transom and the nave. Even the odd familiarity of dusty statues were a link to the past.

To the people I'd loved. The places I'd been. It was a feeling I found hard to explain.

I wasn't religious, necessarily. Although I was raised Catholic, I'd stopped attending Mass with any kind of regularity a long time before. When I was in my early twenties, I served as a Jesuit Volunteer in Montana and lived in a community of women who were dedicated to lives of social justice. It was a time when the connection between faith and life seemed so clear, when I felt fed by my faith. But over the years, I'd grown distant from the practices that once meant so much to me.

The older I got, the more I struggled to reconcile the teachings of the Catholic Church with the practices of its people, particularly the clergy. I found it hard to ignore the damage the church had done to so many. There was the history of violence towards indigenous peoples and the child sex abuse scandals. The blatant homophobia and lack of compassion it seemed to show those who were suffering. As the church grew more dogmatic, it moved farther and farther from the focus on social justice that had drawn me to it. And without a community to feel connected to like the one I'd had earlier in my life; it was hard to want to stay engaged. Now I showed up like the other lapsed Catholics, at Christmas and at Easter, always with the intention that I would get back to attending more frequently, but it never happened. Although I'd never lost my belief in God, I no longer had a structure in which to practice my faith.

The Camino was a religious pilgrimage, even though many now walked for other reasons. Although I hadn't thought much about that aspect of the journey, I promised myself I would stay open to as many opportunities as possible.

The church in Roncesvalles was beautiful. Stone archways enclosed the nave. Tall stained-glass windows framed the sanctuary. A limestone canopy floated above the altar. I looked around, smiling at a few faces I recognized from the day's walk. As the Mass began, a dozen priests, many of whom were walking the Camino themselves, joined the celebrant at the altar.

After Mass, the priest called the pilgrims to the front of the church to receive the traditional blessing, first in Spanish and then in English.

> *"Be for us our companion on the walk, Our guide at the crossroads, Our breath in our weariness, Our protection in danger, Our albergue on the Camino, Our shade in the heat, Our light in the darkness, Our consolation in our discouragements, And our strength in our intentions."*

The priest's words settled around me like a well-worn blanket, a reminder of something I once knew. I'd always been a sucker for poetic metaphor. Somewhere inside me, buried deep in the recesses of my being, something stirred. A connection to something I'd felt a long time ago.

By nine o'clock, with the light still bright in the summer sky, I was ready for sleep. I put on my nightgown, lay my fanny pack on the ledge behind me and crawled into bed.

I awoke to the sound of chamber music playing over the loudspeakers. I rolled over and checked my watch. It was 6:00 a.m. Time to get up. I dressed quickly. Washed my face, brushed my teeth and gathered up my things.

My body registered the moment before my brain could comprehend what had happened. My fanny pack was missing, the bag that held my wallet, passports and credencial. I scoured the area again, pulling up the thin mattress from the frame and checking beneath it. I looked around the floor. I double checked the locker behind me. As each moment passed, my throat tightened, my heart beat harder in my chest. I emptied out my pack again, just in case I had accidently stuffed it inside. Nothing. The small bag was nowhere to be found. I grabbed my pack and walked quickly down the stairs.

The line of people stretched halfway down the hallway. The office was full. The energy chaotic. Voices in different languages reverberated in the cavernous space. The Dutch hospitaleros fanned out, pens and paper in hand. "What's missing?" they asked.

"Everything," said a petite, dark-haired Indian woman across the counter from me, "My passport. My money. My cell phone. It's all gone."

"Mine too." another pilgrim added, this one a man. He was much older, tall, lean, with grey hair and a beard. "I had 1200 euro in my pack."

Money. Credit Cards. Passports. Cell phones. The list grew and grew.

Clearly, I wasn't the only one. As I waited in line, my thoughts spiraled. Had I left it somewhere? I worked backwards, replaying my movements, the way you do when you can't find your car keys. *I'd carried the small blue fanny pack with me into the shower and then to the laundry. I'd paid for the wine so I knew I had it there. Did I have it with me in church? I thought so. Other than in the shower and when I went to sleep, I kept it clipped around my waist. Did I have it when I went to sleep? What would I have done with it? Had I put it down somewhere? On the ledge behind me? On the floor beside my bed?* I couldn't remember. All I knew was that it was gone.

"My fanny pack is missing," I said as I reached the front of the line. A dark-haired woman sat behind the desk, her hair piled on top of her head. Her face was strained, her manicured brows furrowed as she input information into the computer. I could feel my heart pounding in my chest. My US and Italian passports, credit card and bank card. My brand new credencial. Everything that mattered was in there.

"One minute," she said as I described the fanny pack to her. She reached down behind the desk. "Is this yours?"

"Oh thank god," I said, taking it from her, "Thank you so much."

"Someone turned it in this morning. Check the contents. See if everything is there."

Both passports. My credencial. The credit card and my bank card. It was all there. I tried to settle my breath. My hands were trembling.

"What about cash? Did you have any cash?"

I opened the small red wallet I'd purchased specifically for the trip, small enough just to carry what little I'd need. The cash was gone.

The hospitalero shook her head and glanced at her colleague who stood behind her. "How much was in there?" she asked.

"Several hundred euro," I guessed. 400? 500? The truth was, I wasn't sure. I'd taken out money at the bank in Pamplona before I'd boarded the bus to begin the walk. Enough, I'd hoped, to get me through the week. Whatever it was, it was all gone now.

Henrik caught up with me as I was leaving the office, his face flushed with worry. He was the first person I'd told that morning when I realized it was missing. "They found my fanny pack," I said.

"I'm glad. This team has been doing this together for years. Nothing like this has ever happened before," Henrik said, trying to explain. "Everyone who comes in to the albergue must present their credencial. There is no other way to get in. We lock the doors after the pilgrims are in for the night."

"The person who'd robbed us was one of us?" I asked. "Why would someone do this to other pilgrims?" It was so hard to believe.

"It's hard to know. It's probably a group of people. Most likely they came in posing as pilgrims. Everyone has to show their credencial to enter. There's no other way to get in. I've heard about it before, but we've never had to deal with it here."

Overnight, more than a dozen pilgrims were robbed. The hospitaleros called in a local Spanish police detective who advised us to stop in Burguete, the next town we'd pass through, to make a report. But that wasn't all that had been stolen. In the nearby shoe room, someone's *shoes* were missing.

"They were right here," I heard a young woman tell the hospitalero.

"Maybe someone mistook them for theirs?" she said.

"No, hers were green," someone said. "No one could have mistaken them. And she'd left her dirty socks in them. The socks are still there."

Money. Passports. Phones and now someone's shoes.

I grabbed my shoes and found a seat on a bench in the hallway. Although I was relieved to have my bag back, I couldn't shake the feeling that I was somehow to blame. Perhaps I should have been angry. Perhaps I should have felt violated. After all, someone stole something that belonged to me. But instead, I felt embarrassed. I'd been careless. It was my responsibility to make sure my belongings were safe. Behind every bed was a locked cabinet. A place that was designed specifically to keep things safe but I hadn't used it. I'd trusted the people around me. Assumed there was nothing to be fearful of. My decision had been a poor one. For all the traveling I'd done, I should have known better. I'd made a mistake in judgement and now I would pay for my carelessness.

I slid on my shoes and tugged at the laces. A group of pilgrims walked past, heading out for the day's walk. I looked up, and for a minute I found myself wondering if the person in front of me might be the culprit. Or perhaps it was the person behind him? Or the one over there? Suddenly the ground beneath me felt a little less steady. Could I trust the people around me? But almost as soon as I began to go down that rabbit hole, I caught myself. *Let it go, I thought. You were lucky. It could have been a lot worse. It was just money. You have your passports. Your bank card. You're going to be OK.*

I wasn't going to allow myself to feel suspicious. It was a waste of time. It was over and done with and I needed to stop beating myself up. I'd made a mistake. I needed to learn from it and move on. The truth was, I *was* lucky. I had the resources to keep going and I'd be OK just as soon as I could get to a bank. Others had lost much more. I hoped they too would be able to continue.

Still it was an inauspicious start to a journey I'd been looking forward to for months. I'd gone into that first night in Roncesvalles wide open. Perhaps even a little naïve, but I was filled with a trust in the people I was on this journey with. I didn't know them. I didn't really have any reason to trust them, and yet I had. It was the way I'd always tried to live my life, wide open. Whole hearted. It was the only way I knew how to do it. Sure, there'd been times in my life when I'd been hurt. When the people I'd put my trust in let me down and I'd struggled to understand why. And yet, I clung desperately to the belief that people were good. That honesty mattered. That vulnerability would be rewarded. Even when there was evidence to the contrary. I couldn't live any other way.

With only what I could carry on my back, I already felt a paring down, a simplification I had not anticipated. I'd spent so much time getting ready. Hours researching and shopping for all the best equipment. All that stuff I thought I couldn't live without. But in the end, it was just that, stuff. Nothing was so important that it couldn't be replaced. It was all replaceable. Even my passport.

I'd come to the Camino looking to step away from the trappings of daily life. I knew I needed to slow down. To free myself from my reliance on things. To quiet the noise of the world I lived in so I could take the time to listen. The robberies were a reminder. The Camino wasn't about the things in my pack, the beds I would sleep in or the money in my wallet. The Camino was an opportunity to focus on the present. The chance to be right here, right now. To meeting new people. To making friends. The gift of the Camino was the journey. Today was just another step along the way.

I slipped my backpack on my back and walked out into the hall to look for Debbie and Pat. They were adding a few more things to the donation pile.

"What are you going to do?" they asked.

"What I came here to do," I said. What we'd *all* come here to do. "I'm going to keep walking."

DAY 3
ZUBIRI
KILOMETER 47

CHAPTER 3

Acts of Kindness

Before I left Roncesvalles, I found a few remaining euro in the bottom of my pants pocket and bought a cup of coffee from the vending machine, a sad substitution for the rich café con leche I was already beginning to look forward to each morning. Debbie, Pat and I left the monastery a few minutes later, vowing to find breakfast along the way. I was growing fond of them. They were easy to be with, and after just one day, I could already feel myself starting to depend on them.

A few kilometers down the road, we came upon a large outdoor cafe just as we entered the town of Burgette. Nearly every table was filled with pilgrims and backpacks and the buzz of conversation.

I said hello to David, one of the people I'd met the first day on the walk over the Pyrenees and a couple others from the night before in Roncesvalles. David was from Mexico City. We'd walked the first 8 kilometers together to Orisson, chatting about his imminent move to New York City to take a new job. David's English was great, and while I huffed and puffed, he kept the flow of conversation going. He sat at a table with a group of younger pilgrims, younger than me that is, whose faces I'd seen along the way. Some of whom I'd even greeted with the traditional "Buen Camino" as they passed me on the climb. Although I didn't yet know their names, there were others I'd recognized at Mass, or while we rehydrated at the bar or that first night at the communal dinner. One day in, the outline of our Camino cohort was already beginning to take shape. I nodded my head and gave them a broad smile as I walked by.

Let's stop here," Pat said. "You grab a table, and I'll go get us coffee. Do you want something to eat?"

"Oh no," I said. I didn't have any money. I would wait until I could find a bank.

"Are you sure?" Debbie asked. "Let us get you something to eat."

I hesitated for a moment, a silent debate raging in my head. Asking for help had always been hard for me, even from people I knew really well. Still, my stomach was growling and we had a long walk ahead of us. "OK," I said after what seemed like several minutes. "I'll pay you back as soon as I find an ATM."

The screen door slapped behind him as Pat stepped inside. Debbie and I dropped our packs beside an empty table and sat down. When Pat returned a few minutes later, he had a tray with freshly squeezed orange juice, café con leche, yoghurt and a couple of chocolate filled croissants that soon became a staple each morning. I dipped the croissant into my coffee and took a bite, grateful that I'd gotten over the reluctance to ask for help. We had 22 kilometers ahead of us, and although the walk was supposed to be easier than the day before, it undoubtedly would have been more difficult on an empty stomach.

Behind us, a group of pilgrims were discussing the robberies in Roncesvalles. "Shoes? Who steals someone's shoes?"

"Well that's the end of her Camino."

"Maybe not. I heard that the hospitaleros offered to drive her into town and buy her another pair."

I was surprised by how quickly word spread, like the childhood game of telephone. But with nothing but time as we walked for hours, sharing stories was what we did. We had no history with each other. Every moment brand new. Each day was a walking meditation. What mattered was the present moment. Our stories were being written as we walked.

The path meandered through dense forest. Dappled sunlight painted a gentle mosaic on the wooded trail. Rocks jutted out from the earth below and we stepped carefully, planting our feet solidly on the ground. Debbie lagged behind, the weight of her pack making each step difficult. Pat and I walked together, taking turns pulling ahead and then waiting for Debbie to catch up. Somewhere along the way we met a man walking with his two sons.

Oklahoma, as I came to refer to him, was a soft-spoken Midwesterner. He was lean, with dark features and a weathered complexion from time spent outdoors. He was a salt-of-the-earth kind of guy. He'd twisted his ankle the first day, a story that had already made its way along the Camino grapevine.

There'd been some concern that it might keep him from continuing, but overnight the swelling had gone down and he was determined to make it, no matter how long it took him.

Oklahoma had two sons, Hayden and Quinn, both in their 20s. While Quinn, the younger of the two strode on ahead, Hayden kept an eye on his father. His backpack was weighted down with all sorts of photographic equipment. He was the family photographer and it was his job to chronicle the family adventure. Like their father, the boys were outgoing and easy to talk to.

This was their second time on the Camino, Oklahoma told me as we walked along. They'd walked five years earlier, that time with his wife, the boys' mother, who suffered from multiple sclerosis. "She was in a wheelchair," he told me. "It was her dream to walk the Camino." They'd set out to make it come true.

"I saw a documentary about a man who'd pushed his wheelchair bound best friend along the Camino," I said. I remembered being moved by the extraordinary effort required to complete such a journey.

"We met them," he said. "They were filming that at the same time we were here with my wife. They had a big crew with lots of people. We were in some of the original footage. Unfortunately, we didn't make it into the film." He laughed.

I had my own experience with life in a wheelchair. In the final year of my father's life, he too had been confined to a wheelchair. My father had always been an independent man, the foundational rock of our family. He'd provided us with food and shelter, helped me with my homework, and walked me down the aisle. Yet it took less than a year for the ALS to strip him of his independence, from mowing the lawn and playing 18 holes of golf to a man who needed help just to get into bed.

I remembered the effort it took to help him navigate his world. The new awareness I had of ramps and elevators and safety bars that were meant to help accommodate people like him and the limitations and challenges it presented when there were none. But my father refused to let his challenges with mobility limit him. My father was a scientist. A researcher. A thinker. When I was a child, I believed there was nothing he couldn't do. No problems he couldn't solve. Where some saw challenges, he saw opportunities. His solutions weren't always pretty, but he was never afraid to try them. He was willing to tackle anything and if he ever felt uncertain about the challenges ahead of him, he never let on. Even from his wheelchair, my father didn't think in terms of limitations.

Now, as we walked along I found myself paying closer attention to the ground beneath us. The unevenness of the path's surface. The way the trail widened and narrowed. The steep inclines that gave way to rocky descents. I imagined how difficult it must have been for them to make this journey together. The determination and commitment it required. In my years as a social worker, I'd seen that same dedication in my clients, many of whom faced challenges I could only imagine. I watched as they tripped and fell. While some gave up, most of them picked themselves up and kept going. That's what Oklahoma and his family had done. Despite the inevitable challenges life handed them, they kept going. Their resilience and love was inspiring. To bear witness to the courage of the human spirit was nothing short of extraordinary. No matter how many times I saw it, I never took it for granted.

As the path began to descend, the air was filled with the sound of leaves rustling in the breeze. I could hear running water in the distance. Still nursing that sore ankle, Oklahoma walked slowly, planting his feet carefully. At the bottom of the hill, we came to a stream of rushing water that cut the path in half. His sons, who had gone ahead, were waiting there. Seated in the sunshine, they'd shed their packs and dipped their toes in the ice-cold water. Oklahoma and I quickly did the same.

The frigid water numbed my feet and within a few seconds they began to sting. I stepped back, waiting for the pain to subside as I warmed them against the smooth, sun-kissed rock. Despite the harsh temperature of the water, with the sun beating down on us and the sweat pouring down my face, the moment felt like a gift.

"Do you want a banana?" Oklahoma asked. He pulled a piece of fruit out of his pack to offer me one.

"Thanks," I said. It'd been several hours since we'd eaten breakfast and I was really starting to get hungry.

We stood in the shade eating our bananas and watched as people traversed the stream. There were only two ways to get across. One was straight through the water. The other was to walk across a series of concrete pylons set a few feet apart. Both would be a challenge. A group of cyclists raced down the hill and rode straight through, sending a sheet of water into the air. Just as the last one passed, his tire slipped on the wet concrete. His bike slid out from beneath him and dumped the rider into the water. Without hesitation, Hayden and Quinn jumped up and lifted the rider and his bike from the rushing stream.

The pylon option seemed like a better one. I watched as several groups of pilgrims navigated the series until I thought I had it figured out. I made my way onto the first pylon and steadied myself to take the next step. Oklahoma handed me my pack and I found my way across. He followed right behind. In a wheelchair, the only way across was through.

It was hard to imagine making this journey in a wheelchair. Only two days in I'd already seen the variation of terrain, from paved thoroughfares to dirt trails, from gentle paths to vertical climbs in the blink of an eye. With the heat beating down on us and the lack of shade, it was hard enough to manage on your own. I wondered how they'd done it.

"People were really helpful," he said. "You think that you're going to have to do it all yourself. You plan for that. You do the research. You think it through, but help came from everywhere."

For years I'd been teaching a class in active listening. I usually started out my lecture by sharing a Chinese character which is created from a series of words that make up the elements necessary to listen; *ears, eyes, mind, heart and undivided attention. Ears*, I would tell my students, allow us to hear, not just the words, but the tone, pace and emphasis. Listening was more than just the words spoken. We needed to understand the relationship that the words have to the speaker. Our *eyes* allowed us to form connection. When we see the person speaking to us, we pick up on the nonverbal. Our *minds* allowed us to consider what we hear, to learn new information and connect it to our own experiences or expand beyond what we already know. We use our *hearts* to hold compassion. To receive the emotion of the story being shared and in turn build connection with the speaker. And finally, and perhaps the most important I tell them, is in the gift of presence, of *undivided attention*. We must create space for one another. Put aside the noise of the monkey mind and truly be.

In the quiet of the forest, far away from the dozens of things that so often distracted me, I found it easier to listen. A stillness settled in and as we walked along, time seemed to slow down. As I turned to look at him I was struck by how ordinary he seemed. His hair flecked with gray. His skin weathered by the sun. The cotton t-shirt and cargo shorts hung loosely from his lean body. Just a father hiking with his two sons. Unlike the film I'd seen, there'd been no one to document their journey. Theirs was an ordinary one, just a family walking together.

And yet that's what made it so extraordinary. Their path had not been easy. I was struck by this family's dedication to one another. Of the commitment they'd made to each other. They'd turned his wife's dream of walking the Camino into a reality. One of many, I imagined. His was a family that showed up when they were needed. Who followed through on their promise to one another. A family toughened by the resilience of living an ordinary life. Sadly, a few years after they walked the Camino, she'd passed away. Before she died, she'd asked them to promise to take her ashes to Santiago so here they were, five years later, making good on that promise.

She was with him, as he walked along. In the way his eyes sparkled when he mentioned her name. She was with him in the faces of their sons, in the playful banter of a family drawn closer by the struggles they'd endured. She was there in the life they'd built, in the family they created together. She was with him on this journey too.

After a long morning in the hot sun, everyone was ready for lunch. We found a small café at the top of a hill. Debbie, Hayden, Quinn and I grabbed a table while Oklahoma and Pat got in line for food. But despite the fact that my stomach was growling, I still had not found a bank. Although I had a credit card, most places dealt in cash along the Camino. The cafes. The albergues. The food vendors along the way. Everything was cash, and the café was no different. As hungry as I was, I would just have to wait.

"You're getting really sunburned," I said to Hayden as we sat waiting for the guys to come back with the food. He was fair skinned and his face, neck and shoulders were beginning to resemble a ripe peach. "Don't you have a hat?"

His brother laughed. "Hayden was in charge of packing the hats. Of course, he brought one for everyone except himself."

I'd bought a purple, floppy-brimmed, sunhat from REI right before I left. It was an afterthought really, as I wasn't a hat wearer. Nevertheless, I thought I'd be smart and get one for the long stretches that were to come along the meseta. I pulled the hat from my pack and offered it to him. "Take this," I said.

"Thanks," he said, pulling it on his head and letting the tie strings dangle to his shoulders. "This is really going to help."

I smiled. I liked that he didn't seem to mind that it was a woman's hat. It was brand new. I hadn't worn it yet, but it was clear Hayden needed it more than I did. I'd get it back at some point, I thought.

A few minutes later, Oklahoma and Pat appeared with bocadillos and ice-cold drinks for everyone. Including me. "Thank you," I said. "Who do I owe?"

"Don't worry about it," Oklahoma said.

"Thanks." I said again, "But I'd really like to pay you back. That is, when I'm able to get some money."

"No really," he said, waving me off. Yet, despite his objections, I vowed to pay him back just as soon as I could.

As grateful as I was to be taken care of by my newfound friends, I couldn't shake the discomfort I felt for being in the position to need it in the first place. I was raised to be self-sufficient, to stand on my own two feet. I didn't ask for help often. Feeling vulnerable wasn't easy. I felt a certain shame in needing help, especially when it came to money.

I couldn't see it at the time, but there was a certain irony to being unable to receive their generosity. As a social worker, I'd built a career on helping others. I was grateful for the opportunity to give, to share what I had to support someone else.

I certainly didn't think less of the people I worked with for needing help. Why, wasn't that also true for me?

"Help came from everywhere," Oklahoma had said to me. I thought about what might have happened if they'd refused that help. They'd planned to walk the Camino alone. They could have done it alone, but they didn't need to. The kindness they received was a gift, one that made their journey easier.

Lately I've been thinking about a question I was asked many years ago. When I was in my early years as a social worker my mentor had asked, "What do you do when someone gives you a gift?" The answer, he said, was simple. You open it. You accept what is offered.

As I thought about Oklahoma's journey, I was reminded once again that we are not alone in this world. There are people all around us, people who have gifts to offer. Sometimes we're the helper. Sometimes we're the person needing the help. That's the way life works. We all have the capacity to reach out. To listen. To share stories. To connect. We are all in this together and help is out there. It just takes the courage to be vulnerable and the willingness to receive.

We walked the rest of the day together. The more we talked, the more my heart swelled with gratitude. Oklahoma had given me a little window into his life. Theirs had been a unique journey. His wife had been in a wheelchair for much of their life together. Even through raising their children. Despite the inevitable hardships, his story was one filled with selflessness and love. "You should write about it," I encouraged him. Having just spent the past few years writing about my own loss, I knew it would be helpful to him.

"I have done some writing," he said. "I kept a blog for a long time, but I haven't written in a while."

"It really is an amazing story," I said. "I think it's one you need to share." I recounted my own process with him. About how writing about my own experiences had allowed me to see things I'd not seen before. How it had helped me finally heal the grief I could not seem to let go of. I hoped that he would consider it once he returned home.

By the time we reached Zubiri, it was late in the afternoon. After a long walk in the stifling heat, the boys went off to find a bar to get something cold to drink. I still needed to find a bank so I said goodbye to Oklahoma and walked into town, assuming I'd see them again tomorrow. But it didn't work out that way. In fact, I never saw them again.

There is a saying you hear when you walk The Way, 'The Camino provides'. Although it may not give us what we want, it gives us what we need. Five years before, when Oklahoma and his family walked the Camino for the first time, they learned quickly that they were not alone. Despite the difficulties they faced along the way, there were people there to help them. To navigate the rocky terrain, carry his wife's wheelchair across the stream, or pull it from the mud. People to lighten the load. That day, and in the days to come, I would learn that the same would be true for me.

For the rest of the journey, I thought about Oklahoma. From time to time, I still do. I wonder if he ever made it to Santiago and if his son still has my hat.

Journal Entry

Day 3 - Zubiri – Pamplona

21.1 kilometers (13.1 miles) In Zubiri, we stayed at an albergue on the edge of town. The albergue Suseia. The hospitalero greeted us with ice cold lemonade, a welcome relief after a long, hot day of walking. For dinner she made us a wonderful homemade gourmet dinner of a composed salad of the freshest greens, fruit and grains, a delicious chilled gazpacho, albondigas (meatballs) in a rich tomato sauce, and a sweet custard garnished with homemade jam and seeds.

We sat around a long table. Debbie, Pat and I, Martina and Itzy, a couple from New Zealand, two women from Romania and a Scotsman. It was an incredible ending to an amazing day.

DAY 4
PAMPLONA
KILOMETER 68.1

CHAPTER 4

Mothers and Sons

"Rugby is a little bit like your American football, only we don't use helmets or pads," Hugh said as we walked along. The dirt path on the way to Pamplona was edged in floral sprays of deep yellow scotch broom. Clusters of wild roses dotted the landscape. A curious group of sheep poked their noses through wire fencing to say hello.

I'd seen him a day earlier, walking with the Franciscan priest from Philadelphia whose tattered grey robes were hard to miss. Hugh was handsome, solidly build with creamy white skin, a mop of curly brown hair and a gentle brogue. He was young, about the age of my sons. A professional rugby player from Dublin, he was one of a number of Irish pilgrims I'd met in the first few days of walking. They seemed to gravitate towards one another like a school of fish. There certainly seemed to be a lot of them.

I was an avid baseball fan who could hold her own in conversations where sports were concerned. In addition to baseball, I knew a fair amount about basketball, American and European football (the thing we Americans called soccer) and that knowledge had served me well over the years when it came to carrying on a conversation. But rugby was outside my wheelhouse. Many years before, when I was a college student studying abroad, I'd been to a match or two. I still remembered the thrill of standing amongst the fans decked in brightly colored scarves that denoted team allegiance and the singing of the crowd as they cheered their team. But to be honest, when it came to the game itself, I had no idea what I was watching.

"My son, Tucker, played football at university," I said. "He played on the offensive line."

"A big guy, then?"

"Yes. He's 6'5" I don't know what that is metric. But yes, he's a big guy. It took me a long time to get comfortable with him playing. He started in high school. I was a typical worried mother. I didn't want him to get hurt, but somehow he and his father convinced me that it was going to be OK."

Hugh smiled. "And was it?"

"In the beginning, yes, but by the time he got to college, things changed for me. I loved the camaraderie of youth sports. The way the families came together to cheer on their sons and daughters. The team barbecues and post-game celebrations. But sports at the university level were different. The expectations were higher. The competition more intense. The potential for injury is greater too." In four years of playing, he spent a good amount of time on the sidelines. A high school Achilles tear that never seemed to heal. Ankle strains, shoulder damage, and more concussions than he ever admitted to. "It was hard to watch him get hurt." I said, "Now, years after he finished playing, he jokes that he has the body of an old man."

"Football is far more violent," Hugh said. "Although people get injured in rugby. I think the helmets and pads that American football players wear give them a false sense of protection. It's like they use their bodies as weapons."

"I teach psychology for a living," I said. "There's so much research on head trauma coming out right now." The damage done to the brain from post concussive syndrome and chronic traumatic encephalopathy (CTE) were some of the things I talked about with my students, particularly when I lectured on the brain. So many of them had residual damage from concussions they'd suffered. Headaches. Trouble focusing. Memory problems. In recent years there'd been a lot of attention paid to the damage caused by repetitive brain trauma to professional football players and the research was devastating. After being a fan for so many years, it had really soured me on the sport. I wondered if rugby was similar.

"There are injuries in rugby, of course," he said. "But we don't use our bodies the same way, so there's not as many head injuries."

For my son, the challenge of playing a sport while attending university had been a difficult one. The struggle to maintain his studies while spending hours in training and on the field wasn't easy. Still, he'd made connections to his teammates that would likely last a lifetime and as difficult as it was, he'd learned a lot about himself through the experience. I wondered what it was like to be a university athlete in Ireland.

"Oh, I don't play rugby for my university." he explained. The system was different in Ireland. If I understood him correctly, Hugh was in a professional developmental league, one that required that he live away from his family as he trained. His academic classes were coordinated with his team.

As we walked along and bantered back and forth, it was hard not to think about my oldest son. The truth was, I'd been thinking about both of my boys for days now. It seemed like every day something or someone reminded me of one of them.

Of all the things I'd done in my life, being a mother was by far the most meaningful. I remembered each of their births like they were yesterday and the days since then seemed to have come and gone in the blink of an eye. I was 32 when I had Tucker. By then I'd built a career as a social worker and family therapist. But I was unprepared for the depth of my love for him and for a growing desire to give it all up so I could stay home to be with him. And yet, I loved my job and the people I worked with and living in California was expensive. We needed my income, and while the work I did was fulfilling, the tug was constant. There were times when I'd just stare at him, my heart feeling as if it might burst, as though it couldn't hold the emotion I felt inside. Tucker was an easy baby. He rarely cried. He seemed to adapt and adjust to his surroundings effortlessly, and as I watched him grow, I was filled with awe. He was smart, funny and affectionate, and I marveled at his every move.

When I got pregnant with Dylan, I worried that I wouldn't feel the same way about him as I did with his brother. I didn't think my heart could expand enough to allow another being in, but I was wrong. From the minute I held Dylan in my arms, I knew I'd worried for nothing. He was different from his brother.

Dylan was sensitive. He struggled with transitions. The things that worked for his brother didn't work for him. He was difficult to soothe and clung to me like his life depended on it, but over time he taught me how to be the kind of mother he needed me to be.

As I thought back on those years, I realized how lucky we'd been. Although I hadn't appreciated it at the time, we'd made it through unscathed for the most part. I'd labored through every unexpected twist and turn. Without the wisdom that distance brings, I'd spent my share of sleepless nights and shed plenty of tears. My heart broke when my boys were treated unfairly. When things didn't go as they'd hoped. I hated to see them disappointed. I wanted to make it right. Sometimes I even tried. If I allowed myself to think about it, the depths of my love for them frightened me. I could not imagine my life without them, and the desire to defend and protect them welled up within me. It was all I could do to keep it in check.

And still, we'd avoided the pain some of our friends had gone through. Our children were healthy. They were smart, compassionate and caring. Even in the teenage years, when navigating the waters of adolescence were so dangerous, their problems were minor. We'd had a relatively smooth sail. They'd both graduated from college and were on their own, making their way in the world. It was hard not to be proud of them.

But their transition to adulthood had not been an easy one for me, particularly when it came to my oldest. As he launched into a life of his own, I grappled with my own expectations. I wanted to circumvent the struggle inherent in self-discovery, to offer "guidance" in the hopes of being "helpful", but all it seemed to do was push him farther away. He felt judged and pushed to pursue a path he believed I had chosen for him.

I suppose it shouldn't have been a surprise. As the oldest, I too had walked a tightrope of expectations, the weight of which, at times, felt like an albatross around my neck. I'd done all I could to make my mother proud of me and still never felt like I'd succeeded. I longed for a friendship with her, a give and take that could allow me to be myself in her presence. But it never happened. As an adult I spent years frustrated, struggling to make sense of a disappointing relationship with her. I didn't want that to be my legacy with my son.

As I walked along with Hugh, I asked about his family. He answered thoughtfully. They were a close family, he'd said, telling me a little bit about his siblings. His love for his family was evident. Living away during training, he didn't get to see them as much as he wanted although he talked to them regularly. In fact, it was his parents who encouraged him to walk the Camino. I was touched by the ease in our back and forth. Despite our obvious age difference, there was a gentle give and take of conversation. Without the burden of expectations, it was easy to be curious. I wondered what it might be like if I could practice the same with my own son.

We came across an old stone church in Zabaldica and took off our packs to go inside. A habit-clad nun, her fine grey hair peeking out from underneath her coif, greeted us as we entered. She invited us to sign the registry and stamp our credencial. Hugh wandered up to the bell tower and I fished out a couple of euro and lit a candle in memory of my mother and father, something I'd begun doing that first day in St-Jean. It was a simple ritual, but it reminded me to keep them with me as I walked. Somehow, lighting a candle made me feel like I was leaving a little bit of them along the way.

"I'm starting to get hungry," I said after he came down. "I was hoping we'd find some food here."

"It doesn't look like it. Let's keep walking. Hopefully we'll find something along the way."

Just outside the town of Pamplona we stopped for lunch. We joined a group of pilgrims at an outdoor table for four, one that quickly expanded well beyond its boundaries. It was always such a joyous chaotic scene. Backpacks and walking sticks everywhere. Pilgrims soaking up the midday sun. Slices of tortilla, glasses of orange juice, bocadillos de jamon and a few chocolate croissants filled plates perched awkwardly on whatever flat surfaces were available. The hum of enthusiastic conversation filled the air.

The sound of drumming pierced the symphony of pilgrims' voices. Moments later a parade of townspeople dressed in white shirts and blue bandanas filled the streets. They carried giant puppets of kings and queens that towered high into the air. A small band of musicians followed along, accompanying them. The puppets spun in time with the squeal of instruments, twirling round and round as they passed before us.

"Come on," I said to Hugh as I jumped up from the table. I'd seen parades like this before when I lived in Barcelona. *Gigantes*, the Spaniards called them. I pushed through the crowd to get a closer look.

After the parade passed we continued on, arriving in Pamplona around two in the afternoon, We found our way to the municipal albergue *Jesus y Maria* in the center of town. Compared to some of the others I'd stayed in, this albergue was enormous, with long, corridor-like rooms filled with seemingly endless rows of metal bunk beds. Hugh and I were assigned bunks next to each other about halfway down the row in the first dormitory. But much to my disappointment, they were both top bunks. I took a quick glance at the vertical metal ladder that looked like it might collapse under the weight of my body. "I'm too old for this stuff," I groused.

Hugh laughed. "I'm going to find my suitcase," he said.

It had been a source of teasing earlier in the day. For a small fee it was possible to transport your bag from town to town. The "send on folks" were easy to spot. While most of us wielded backpacks stuffed to the gills, they carried small day packs. "Real" pilgrims tied spare shoes to the outside of their packs and hung wet socks from the webbing to dry in the midday sun. While we labored up and over the Pyrenees with 20 kilos on our backs, the "send on" crowd looked as if they were out for a Sunday stroll. Hugh was an athlete. Certainly there was no reason for him to send his bag on. Except that he did.

"My mother told me that everyone sends their bag on," he said. "When she and my dad walked the Camino, that's what they did. I just assumed she knew what she was talking about."

"That'll teach you to believe everything your mom tells you," I teased.

I loved the ease with which we joked back and forth, the banter between us. Age seemed irrelevant. Any sense of initial discomfort quickly disappeared. Like the other people I'd encountered since the walk began, it didn't seem to matter that we'd just met, it was as if we'd been friends for years. There was hardly an awkward moment between us.

That night I climbed up to the top bunk and lay on my back. Still fully clothed, I stared at the ceiling. The first two nights on the Camino I'd felt comfortable enough to change into my pajamas, but in a room with so many people and an abject lack of privacy, I wasn't about to do that here. Three days in, I still hadn't managed to get a full night of sleep. Soon after the lights went out, the man in the bottom bunk began to snore. I looked over at Hugh, his face lit up by the glow of his cell phone. "Good night," I said. I didn't imagine either one of us would be getting much sleep tonight either.

Early the next morning, I slid awkwardly down the metal ladder and landed with a thud on the concrete floor. No sooner had they turned on the lights when I heard the sound of ruffling bedsheets, the zipping and unzipping of backpacks and the familiar wishes of 'Buen Camino' that became a symphony each morning as pilgrims headed out for the day.

I walked over to the vending machines and bought myself a cup of coffee. I wasn't sure how much sleep I'd gotten, but I knew it wasn't a lot. Between the chorus of snoring, the staleness of an overstuffed room and the concentration of smells from dozens of pilgrims packed in like sardines, it had been a long night. I went off to check in with Debbie and Pat while Hugh left to take care of making arrangements to send his bag on. I found them sitting on their bunks, their belongings spread out around them.

"We're consolidating," Pat said. "We have too much stuff." In the first few days of the Camino, Debbie was struggling. To make matters worse, she'd twisted her knee and the weight of the pack was making it more difficult. It made sense to pare down. I'd gone with them the night before to find a smaller day pack for Debbie. Pat would carry the bulk of the weight and they'd send what was left to the hotel they'd booked in Santiago.

I was struck by how protective he was towards her, how often he checked on her to see how she was doing. Debbie and Pat were a team. *DebbieandPat.* A singular unit, as if there was no space between them. As I watched their interactions with each other, I couldn't help but wonder what it might be like to walk with Bob, how we might handle making this journey together. But we were two very different individuals. Bob and I were both oldest children. We could be headstrong and opinionated. I was an extrovert who thrived on the electricity of human interaction. He was the eternal introvert, happy to spend his time reading books.

But that wasn't the only thing. Bob was more inclined towards the *we*. To operate as a team. I, on the other hand, struggled to assert my independence. To be seen as separate individuals, an issue left over from my childhood. I could be intolerant and unforgiving. I was struck by Pat's generosity with Debbie. The way his first instinct was to consider her. As hard as it was to admit, I knew I wouldn't have been as considerate as Pat was.

An hour later Hugh caught up with me on the trail. Today's walk would take us up over Alto de Perdón to Puente La Reina, 23.8 kilometers (14 miles) away. I looked forward to reaching the metal sculptures of medieval pilgrims that looked over the valley at Alto de Perdón, one of the few landmarks I'd anticipated seeing. After yesterday's lesson on the game of rugby, we'd moved on to talking about other things. I learned about what he was studying in college. More about his family and some of the places he'd traveled. While I had weeks of walking ahead of me, this would be his last day on the Camino. After Puente la Reina he would be leaving to join a friend in Bilbao for a few days before heading home.

Windmills dotted the ridge before us. For a moment I was transported back in time when, as a child, I'd visited La Mancha with my family. We'd retraced the steps of Don Quixote while my mother recounted the story of the errant knight who did battles with windmills to defend the honor of his beloved Dulcinea. More than forty years later, I could still hear my mother singing to us as we drove down the road in our rented van. *Dulcinea... Dulcinea...I see heaven when I see thee, Dulcinea, And thy name is like a prayer an angel whispers... Dulcinea... Dulcinea!*

We took pictures in front of the sculpture at the top of the mountain, enlisting a Canadian pilgrim to take a few shots of Hugh and me together. I would send them off to my kids as soon as I had the chance. I knew they'd get a kick out of seeing their mom with an Irish rugby player.

The path down from Alto de Perdón was steep and very rocky. I stood at the top, trying to assess the best way to go. I decided to approach it as if I were skiing down a mountain, planting my poles in the ground and zig zagging my way across the terrain. It was hard to stay upright. The rocks rolled under my feet and I felt unsteady. I'd take a dozen steps and then prop myself up for a minute or two to regain my balance until I was ready to begin again. My ankles twisted on the loose rocks as they gave way beneath me. Ahead of me, Hugh traversed the hillside with ease, pausing every now and then to look back and make sure I was still okay.

Halfway down a sharp pain began to emanate from deep inside my left ankle. I looked ahead to gauge how much farther I had to go. Nothing but a river of rocks as far as the eye could see. Fatigue set in. Putting any pressure on my left ankle seemed almost impossible. Giving way to the frustration, I pounded my pole into the ground, hoping to take some of the weight off my left side. For the first time since I began walking the Camino, I began to feel discouraged. I just needed to get to the bottom of the hill.

"Are you okay?" Hugh called from down below.

"I think so," I said. "My ankle is killing me." I continued to move intentionally, talking myself through each step as if willing myself to finish. By the time I got down to the bottom, my shirt was soaked with sweat. My heart pounded in my chest and the pain in my ankle was intensifying. I needed to find a place to sit down.

I limped into a café a few kilometers down the road and sat down to untie my shoe and give my ankle a rest. Hugh fished through his backpack and handed me a couple of Advil, then went inside to get us something to drink. Outside the café was a vending machine with all sorts of medical supplies. I hobbled over, my legs still pulsing from the treacherous decline. I dropped a couple euro in the coin slot and chose what I hoped was an ace bandage. Hugh returned to the table with two glasses of lemonade and a bite to eat while I waited for the Advil to kick in. A little while later I wrapped my ankle tightly, pulled my sock over the bandage and laced up my shoe.

Just as we got ready to head out again, we ran into a couple of young men from Limerick, part of the group of Irishmen I'd met the day before. The four of us took off together, taking turns keeping pace with one another. By then the Advil was working and although I was walking gingerly, I was able to keep up. Suddenly, without any warning, I lost my footing. I fell forward, landing flat on my face in a ditch along the side of the road.

Before I even realized what had happened, I was upright, scooped up by my Irish walking buddies. "Are you okay?" they asked, brushing the gravel from my knees and hands.

"Yes," I said. "Thank you."

"Do you need to rest?" Hugh asked.

"No. I'm alright," I said, taking a quick inventory. My knees were scraped up pretty good and the palm of my hand was starting to bleed, but that was nothing compared to the bruise the fall left on my ego.

I steadied myself and began to walk again. While the Irish banter continued, for me things had changed. I felt exposed. It was as if my fall had uncovered a weakness, something I did not want to see. I judged myself harshly. I hung back, embarrassed and ashamed in my vulnerability.

As we came into town, I said goodbye to Hugh. "Thank you for walking with me," I said. I was so grateful for the time we'd spent together.

"Of course," he said. "If my mother were walking the Camino, I'd want someone to walk with her."

I bristled at his words. Is that how he'd seen me? As a mother? It wasn't the role so much. I loved being a mother. It was an important piece of who I was. Rather, it was the presumed weakness, as if being a mother, *being older*, made me more vulnerable. For a moment it felt like what I had experienced as friendship was instead obligation, time spent together because he felt sorry for me. I didn't want that.

Ever since I'd begun walking, I'd been thinking about the way we defined one another and how often those definitions led to judgements. We identified one another around so many things. Gender. Wealth. Race. Age. It seemed so easy to see people as one-dimensional. Mother or daughter. Old or young. Teacher or student. Social Worker, athlete or pilgrim. I wondered what those identities meant? What power did they hold? How did they limit the way we saw one another? The way we treated one another? How did they shape the way we understood ourselves?

These limitations of identity were what the theologian Henri Nouwen called "The Five Lies of Identity". "I am what I have, I am what I do, I am what other people say or think of me, I am nothing more than my worst moment, I am nothing less than my best moment," he wrote. It was a slippery slope. There was so much tied into the way we saw each other and the way we saw ourselves.

Identities could both enhance and diminish us. They could be the conduit for companionship and connection or the justification for pain and isolation. None of us were singular beings. We were complex, unique individuals and part of an intricate web of connection. To family. Friends. Colleagues and strangers. I was old *and* young. Teacher *and* student. Mother and daughter too. Like most of us, some of my identities were easy to embrace. Others forced me to face truths I'd just as soon deny.

The things we so often used to define one another were irrelevant on the Camino. We did not know one another's history – our jobs, successes or failures - the traditional things that defined us were invisible here. All we knew was the moment. Over and over again I would be reminded of this dilemma, the tendency we had to define one another, to put the people we meet in boxes. To simplify so as to understand. Why did we so often put people into boxes? And why was it so difficult to see people as more than one thing? What are we afraid of? We were complex, multidimensional creatures. How different our lives could be if we just embraced that.

It wasn't the label of mother that I'd reacted to, rather it was the perception that I was vulnerable. That I needed someone to walk with me. To care for me. I'd always prided myself on being independent, able to carry my own weight. Despite being almost 60, I was healthy and fit and I could still do what I wanted. I'd begun this journey to Santiago, and I intended to finish it. I was perfectly capable of doing it alone. I didn't need anyone to walk with me.

But Hugh didn't want me to be alone. "*I'd want someone to walk with her,*" he'd said.

Why had I heard his words as condemnation? Why had I received them as judgement? Rather than a sign of perceived weakness, why could I not see the gift of generosity he was offering me? The respect he was bestowing on me. Sure, I would have been fine on my own. I *was* fine on my own, but hadn't the days walking with him been more interesting, more wonderful, more filled with joy? The companionship he offered me on those days were a gift, not from pity but of kindness. And when I struggled, because I had, as I labored down the rocky slope, as my legs gave out from underneath me, he'd waited, bearing witness to my journey. He'd offered me help, not out of obligation but because he wanted to show me respect, a care and compassion he thought I deserved. Why was that so hard for me to accept?

Why was it so difficult for me to receive help from others? Why did I feel the need to even the score? "I'll pay you back," I'd insisted when my friends bought me lunch. Had the tables been turned, I would have done the same for them. It would have given me great pleasure, in fact. Why was it so difficult for me to allow others that same opportunity?

DAY 5
ESTELLA
KILOMETER 113.7

CHAPTER 5

First Impressions

"I had you pegged as a cougar," Emma said, laughing, She had a broad freckled face and silky blonde hair and her Irish brogue made the comment seem all the more mischievous. "I saw you the first day walking up to Orisson with the young Mexican fella. I figured he was your boyfriend."

Debbie, Pat and I stood in the bustling Café Mundo, searching the room for an open table. My feet were throbbing and all I could think about was sitting down. The room was packed with peregrinos (the Spanish word for pilgrim). Across the expanse of tables, Debbie and Pat spotted a few they'd met on the trail and when a long table opened, we waved them over to join us.

"You what?" I said, as we shuffled our way to a table in the back. "You mean David?" My cheeks flushed with embarrassment. "Oh no," I said without even pausing for a breath. "I just met him that morning."

I thought back to that first day. It seemed so long ago. Now, five days in, I'd settled into a rhythm, but those first few steps would be forever etched in my memory. It was cool that first morning and everything was brand spanking new. The canvas of my steel grey pack was spotless. My Keens only slightly broken in. I pulled a wool overshirt over the baby blue quick-dry tee and sinched up the tie on my camp shorts. The collapsible hiking poles I'd bought at an outdoor shop in Barcelona where I'd stopped for a few days to visit my friend Elena still had the tags on them. I opened the clasp and extended the shaft, estimating a comfortable length for my 5'4" frame. Those first few steps were awkward. I'd never used hiking poles before and walking with them felt like when I learned to ski in high school, unsure of how to get everything to move in the same direction. Within minutes of forging my way through the old town gate, scrums of pilgrims began to pass me on the way up that first incline.

And that's when I met David, the guy Emma mistook for my 'boyfriend'.

David was indeed handsome, with dark brown hair and soulful brown eyes. He was in his early 30's I guessed. "Hola, Buen Camino" I said, trying out my Spanish as he walked up beside me.

"Hola, Como estás?"

"Bien," I said, "Estoy muy emocionada para comenzar." My morning coffee had kicked in and I was filled with rookie enthusiasm.

"Hablas español?"

"Un poquito," I said, not wanting to oversell myself. I could hold my own, that was for sure but despite years of study, I certainly wasn't fluent. I made too many mistakes, confused my tenses and often grew frustrated with my limited vocabulary. Seven years before, when I'd spent a semester teaching in Barcelona, I'd been reticent to speak, too afraid of making a mistake. I promised myself I was going to use my Spanish this time around.

As the path began to climb higher and higher, the paved road gave way to dirt and gravel. I pushed my pace to keep up with my new Camino friend.

"De donde estás?" I asked. *Where are you from?* I was in full Spanglish now, speaking Spanish when I was sure and English to avoid looking foolish.

"Ciudad de Mexico," he said and then, switching to English. "But I am about to move to New York for work. And you?"

"California," I said, "But I grew up in New Jersey." Even though I'd lived in California for more than 30 years, I was still a Jersey girl at heart. "When are you moving to New York?"

"In the middle of July," he said. "I am meeting a friend in Rome on June 29th after I finish the Camino and then I will fly to New York."

"The 29th?" It was June 1st, and almost 500 miles to Santiago. The guidebook said the journey would take anywhere from 30 to 35 days. I couldn't imagine how he was going to finish.

"I worked with a travel guide in Mexico City who mapped it out for me," he said. "I'm going to have some long days, but I think I can do it."

As the path continued to climb, we passed a herd of long haired mountain sheep who seemed undeterred of the constant stream of pilgrims who wandered through the field where they were grazing. David took the climb quickly, his long gait and trim body moved effortlessly while I worked hard to keep up. As we chatted back and forth I gasped for breath, my answers growing briefer and briefer as the climb intensified. Still, I was buoyed by the excitement of the moment. Of the warmth of the sun on my skin. Of the energy of the people around me.

David's new job was in the tech industry. Having already left Mexico City, he was eager to start his life in New York. I wondered if he'd been there before. I imagined he was in for a shock if he hadn't. Despite spending a lot time there as a child, I still found the city overwhelming.

"I have," he said. "I've been to New York many times on business. Mexico City is similar in some ways. It's very busy with lots of people and traffic."

Having set out alone that morning I was so grateful to have someone to walk those first few kilometers with. Now Emma's vivid imagination had turned an innocent walk into a surreptitious affair. "You stopped to take our picture," Emma said, scrolling through the pictures on her cell phone until she located it. "Here."

I had to confess, I hadn't remembered, but there it was.

"And, you know how it is. You see people and you try to guess who they are… what their story is," she joked. "I figured you'd left the husband at home and taken up with a younger man." Emma's broad smile filled her freckled face and her eyes twinkled with a hint of playful wickedness.

"You do?" I said. It hadn't occurred to me to try to figure out anyone's backstory just by looking at them. I shook my head in disbelief. If only she knew how un-cougarlike I really was. "Well, you're half right." I smiled, starting to feel a little more at ease. "I left the husband at home. He's not much for walking."

Although Emma's teasing caught me off guard initially, I wasn't altogether unfamiliar with it. I've always had an affinity for the Irish. Having grown up in an Italian household, I had very little exposure to Irish culture. That is, until I found myself in college in Boston where it seemed like everyone I met was either Irish or Italian. Now, looking back, I realized that many of my dearest friends were descendants of people from the country of Guinness and James Joyce. During my four years there, I'd participated in more than my fair share of St. Patrick's Day celebrations. Irish bars were a mainstay of Boston life, and on St. Patrick's Day people poured out of them into the streets, celebrating like there was no tomorrow.

I'm a pureblood. My mother's father immigrated from Rome as a young man. On the other side I'm Sicilian. My paternal grandfather came to the United States as a child from a small village in central Sicily called Santa Margherita de Belice. I was proud of my Italian pedigree.

But the purity of our family's Italian lineage would not continue. By the time my mother's brother married, the integration of the two cultures began. He married a half Italian, half Irish girl. My father's brother married an Irish girl too. Now, several generations later, Irish blood flows through both sides of my extended family.

And, as it was in college, today the same rang true. Some of my dearest friends are Irish. They are playful and lighthearted, a strong contrast to the emotional intensity of the Italians I knew. And though we had different temperaments, I considered us to be opposite sides of the same coin. We valued family. Were faithful, hardworking and deeply spiritual people. As immigrants, our relatives each had their share of difficulties assimilating into the American culture. And like the Italians, most of the Irish I knew were Catholic.

At the table, we made our introductions. Besides Debbie, Pat, Emma and I there were Tim and Jeanette, the couple from

Adelaide, Australia; Patrick and Maria, a brother and sister from Florida and California, and Emma's husband Conor. They were from Dublin.

While the rest of us were Camino newbies, Conor and Emma were not. Although they'd never walked all the way through, they'd walked sections of the Camino, including the final 100 kilometers, the popular five day stretch from Sarria to Santiago. That was all that was needed to earn the prized compostela, the certificate that marked the completion of the trail. This time they planned to walk for 10 days, from St-Jean-Pied-de-Port to Burgos. The Australians, Tim and Jeanette, only planned to walk as far as Logroño, about 6 days. The rest of us were going all the way.

Emma jumped up from the table and returned with a handful of small, national flags representing each of our countries. Within minutes the conversation grew raucous and everyone was laughing. Emma and Conor played off each other with a timing reminiscent of the classic comedy couples I'd grown up with. Desi Arnaz and Lucille Ball. Jerry Stiller and Anne Meara. They had a way of putting everyone at ease, bantering back and forth with an unabashed teasing that cut through any self-consciousness or timidity that lingered.

We rarely saw each other on the trail. We were early risers. Conor and Emma slept in. While Debbie, Pat and I stayed in pilgrim albergues, Conor and Emma preferred hotel rooms. While we schlepped all our worldly belongings on our backs, Conor and Emma lived out of suitcases that arrived at their hotel long before they would shuffle in. We spent hours teasing them about it, but Emma was fond of reminding us "that everyone walks their own Camino", and this was the way she chose to walk hers.

The Irish folk I met in the early days of the Camino were some of my first friends. Besides Conor and Emma, there was

Hugh and Martin, the boys from Limerick and Irish English John. They seemed to find each other like a swarm of honeybees. After a long day of walking, you could find them glommed together in a pub, lifting pints and telling stories.

I looked forward to seeing Conor and Emma each day. After a long day of walking, Debbie, Pat and I would shuffle into the local pub and there they'd be, sitting at the bar, often flanked by a few of the others. One of the regulars was John, a man Emma dubbed "Irish English John", a nod to his Irish heritage. Despite the fact that he now lived in the middle of England, his family hailed from Ireland. Irish English John was tall and fit with a warm smile, a thick head of grey hair and dark brown eyes. He was somewhere in his mid-sixties and like the other Irish folk, he was easy to talk to. He quickly became part of our expanding Camino family.

It was strange how it happened so quickly on the Camino, this strong connection to people you barely knew, bound together by this experience of walking. With just five days behind me, I'd already met so many people. This was part of the reason I'd wanted to go alone, to open myself to whatever opportunities might present themselves to me.

But as it turned out, I could not anticipate what I would discover. Before I began the journey my focus had been on the walk itself. The miles under my feet. The mountains I might climb. The strain it would take on my body. And that was all there.

But I was quickly learning that the Camino was much more than that. The Camino was about people. That night, as we sat around the table in the back of that little café in Estella, our Camino family was forming, a series of relationships that would expand and grow all the way to Santiago.

Journal Entry

Day 6 - Estella – Los Arcos

21.6 kilometers (13.4. miles) Woke up to the sound of rain hitting the roof of the albergue, an old leather factory that had been converted to a comfortable lodging for pilgrims. Alex and I put on our rain clothes and were on our way. The rain gear worked well, although my new bladder leaked and soaked the inside of my pack.

We made it to the Irache wine fountain around 8:30. As soon as we arrived we realized we didn't have anything to drink out of but there were a group of pilgrims there who were willing to share their plastic cups with us. The wine was young, on the sour side, and not particularly good, but still it was a fun stop. Next door was an ironworker who had a gift shop so we browsed there for a few minutes as well. I thought briefly about buying something, but quickly realized I'd have to carry it to Santiago. I don't need any extra weight.

Day 8
Logroño
Kilometer 163

CHAPTER 6

Reflections

After seven days of walking through small hamlets and villages, the city of Logroño felt like an assault on my senses. The noise in the streets was shocking. Trucks rumbled down the road. Sirens blared and there were people everywhere. The walk into the city was long. The walls of the buildings towered above me like giants. Logroño was a lively city, but the farther I strode into the center, the more I longed for the tranquility outside it, the song of the birds, the fields of poppies, the sun glistening on the stalks of wheat.

In recent days Debbie, Pat and I had been sharing accommodations, but in Logroño they made a reservation in a hotel. Rather than find an albergue on my own, I too decided to look for something similar. I settled on the Hostal La Numantina, a few blocks from the main square. Unlike large hotels, hostals are more often small, family run lodgings with a handful of rooms.

It was not an easy choice. I felt guilty, as if I was somehow "breaking the rules" of the Camino. Before I'd left to begin this journey, my husband encouraged me to "treat" myself from time to time. To take a break from the traditional communal lodging in favor of something more comfortable. I'd recoiled at his suggestion. No hotels for me, I'd told him. The Camino was a pilgrimage. It wasn't meant to be comfortable. In my mind, if I was going to do it, I was going to do it the "right" way.

The hostal was on the second floor of a multi-story building, a few blocks from the main square. After the long walk into Logroño, my feet throbbed. Exhausted, I dragged myself up the wide marble staircase and checked in. The room at the end of the hall was small, barely big enough to contain a double bed, a small armoire, chair and side table, but the crisp white sheets on the bed and the fresh smell in the air felt like an ice-cold glass of water on a hot summer day. I slid off the backpack and let it drop to the floor. I stepped into the bathroom, turned on the shower and peeled off my sweaty clothes. The shower was clean, the water hot and there were real towels. For a week now I had been getting by with something called a travel towel. In truth, it was little more than a car wash shammy and although the package said it was large, it was the size of two dish towels sewn together and just as thin. Not only did it not cover my body, it had not come close to drying it.

As I stood under the shower spigot, I raised my face upwards as if standing in a summer rain. I let the spray wash down my body as I lathered my hair with the free shampoo, taking an extra minute to rinse it out. I used both towels, one to wrap my body and the other around my head, twisting it into a turban and tucking in the edge to hold it in place. It felt luxurious. I put on clean clothes, washed out the ones I was wearing and hung them on a line I'd strung across the small balcony that overlooked the street. I checked my watch. Although it was nearing dinner time, the light still streamed through the window beside the bed. With the nine hour time difference between Spain and California, Bob would just be waking up. I pulled myself up on the bed and placed a video call to my husband. Although I'd been sending him pictures each evening, it was the first time I'd spoken to him since I began walking.

"Hey," I said when he answered. "How are you?"

"Hello. I'm good. How are you? Where are you? How is it going?"

The water from my wet hair began to drip down the front of my shirt. I perched the phone on the pillow and wobbled across the room to grab my hairbrush. "You're walking rather tenderly," he said.

"It's called the Camino shuffle," I said. "Everyone moves like this after a day of walking. By the end of the day your feet are killing you. I'm doing OK, although I'm starting to get a blister on the back of my heel."

"I'm glad you decided to stay in a hotel," he said. "After all that walking, you deserve to treat yourself."

"Thanks," I said. "And thanks for all those messages. I really look forward to them every morning."

Ever since my Camino began, I'd been waking up to texts from him each day. A quick hello or well wishes for the day ahead. Sometimes they came with pictures. Of our dogs, Gracie,

Rusty and Dakota. A new bloom on the ajuga I planted before I left or the first (and only) artichoke in the vegetable garden. With each picture was an encouraging message.

"Well, the dogs and I miss you," he said. "We're so proud of you."

I said goodbye and went off to find something to eat. I didn't know where Debbie and Pat were staying and we hadn't made plans to meet up, so I figured I was on my own for dinner. As I walked, I looked around hoping to see someone I recognized. In the small hamlets of the Camino, the bars and cafes were always full of pilgrims and it was easy to find a face you recognized but here, in the expanse of the big city, I was lost in a sea of strangers. For the first time since I began my journey, I was conscious of being alone.

On the main street leading into the square, I spotted a gaggle of American university students who were gathered at an outdoor café. I'd met a few of them on the first day when they stopped to ask me to take a picture of them on the long climb up to Orisson. I'd seen them a few times since then, when I'd stopped to grab a bite to eat or when they passed me on a long stretch of road. They were hard to miss. The girls' long hair shimmered in the sunlight and the boys, with their lanky bodies, scraggly facial hair and baseball caps, always seemed to be laughing and carrying on. They were a playful bunch.

There were times, as I walked alone, when I'd see them together and I'd catch myself feeling jealous. Times when I longed for company, for the companionship they had. But it had been my choice to come alone, I reminded myself. To give myself the opportunity to experience the Camino unconstrained, without being beholden to others. I'd chosen to walk my own Camino, without the safety net that friends provide. To be open to whatever came my way. To feel whatever came up, even the hard stuff. Whether I had realized it at the time or not, this was the exact reason I'd chosen to come alone.

I walked up and said hello, the sound of my voice muted by uncertainty. I felt like an outsider, the new kid trying to find their footing in a land of well-established friendships. Maria, a neuropsychology student from the University of San Diego, introduced me to the others. "Hi," I said as I smiled awkwardly. I noticed my apprehension, my cheeks flushing with the embarrassment of knowing I was not one of them.

"Sit down and join us," Maria said and motioned to an empty chair. Fighting the urge to give way to my discomfort and decline the invitation, I sat down next to an attractive young blonde named Chloe who, I soon learned, attended Cornell University, where my son went.

"I loved visiting him in college," I said. The Cornell campus was in the picturesque town of Ithaca, in upstate New York. I thought back to summers spent in a rented house on Lake Cayuga, the morning sun glistening on the water. The symphony of pounding water at Taughannock Falls or the crisp fall air of a warm October day during football season when we'd line up to watch the marching band lead my son's football team, The Big Red, into Schoellkopf field before we took our seats in the stands.

"It is such a beautiful campus." Chloe pulled out a cigarette, lit it and took a long drag.

I was taken aback, surprised to see a young person smoking. My maternal instincts kicked in, the way they did sometimes when my college students came to see me during office hours. In the United States in recent years there'd been such a strong emphasis on smoke free environments and healthy living that most people had given it up, at least in my circle of friends. In fact, I didn't know anyone who smoked anymore. In the moment I fought the urge to discourage her, as though my words might have an impact, but we have only just met. Instead, I lean back to avoid the smoke as she exhales in my direction. After a few minutes I excuse myself and continue on in search of something to eat.

The next morning Debbie and Pat tell me that they've decided to take the bus to Nájera. Debbie's knee continues to bother her and she and Pat have chosen to take the day off from walking to give it a chance to rest. For the first time since I began walking in St-Jean, I begin the day alone. We have entered La Rioja, the famous wine region of Spain. Soon there are lush green vineyards dense with young clusters of tempranillo grapes as far as the eye can see. The bright sun rises behind me as I walk and casts a ten-foot shadow in front of me. Ahead of me I see a young man walking. I have seen him before, walking alone. He always walks alone.

"Buen Camino," I said as I approached him. It is the thing we say again and again as we pass one another.

"Buen Camino," he answered, nodding at me.

He is young. His dark hair peaks out from below a large tan sunhat. The straps dangle well below his chin. His eyes are hidden behind inky sunglasses but he smiles when he turns to look at me.

"Good morning." I said. "My name is Suzanne."

"I am Kwang," he said. His accent is unfamiliar, so strong that at first I did not understand him.

"Where are you from?" I asked, hoping he speaks enough English to answer. Although I can make my way in Spanish, it is English that is the universal language on the Camino. Most people speak at least enough to answer a few questions.

"I am from South Korea," he said and I am immediately drawn in.

Kwang tells me that he is 21. "20 in your country." In South Korea, he explains, they begin counting birthdays on the day you are born. Your first birthday is indeed the day of your birth. "It's a little confusing," he said.

"Why are you walking the Camino?" I asked.

"I have just finished my time in the army," he says.

I am struck by his youth. While I know the military is filled with young men and women just like him, there is a realness to this moment. A deeper understanding of the sacrifice we ask our young people to take. I look closely at his face. He is just a boy.

"How long were you in the army?"

"Almost two years," he says. "In South Korea, all young men must join the military."

"In the United States military service is not mandatory," I said. It was 1973, my freshman year of high school, when the draft ended in the United States. While I had students who served in the military, I had very little firsthand experience. My uncle was in the Navy and my husband's father and brother too, but their service ended long before I knew them. They had joined voluntarily. Being forced into service was a completely different matter.

"What was it like?" The words left my mouth before I could stop them. I wondered if he'd seen combat. And yet I was aware that the question itself was a slippery slope. Most of what I knew came from stories I'd heard from my students about their experiences in Afghanistan and Iraq. For many of them, the trauma was still difficult to manage. "It's OK, if you don't want to say," I added. Although I was curious, I didn't want to bring up anything that might cause him pain.

"It was very difficult," he said, his voice stilted as he spoke. "I was on the border. I am very glad to be finished. The whole time I was very scared."

We walked together in silence for a few minutes. The crunch of footsteps in the dirt below us the only audible sound. Around us, hectares of wheat fields rippled in the gentle breeze.

"I wish your president would stop tweeting," he said, finally.

For the previous two years the president of the United States had been engaged in a dangerous game of chicken, tweeting provocations and threats at the ruler of North Korea. In response to the baiting by our government, North Korea began conducting nuclear missile tests which had, in turn, put the South Korean government on edge.

"I wish he would stop tweeting too," I said.

"When I was at the border we went into high alert each time your president tweeted. We were waiting for Kim Jong Un, the ruler of North Korea, to do something that would put us all in danger."

In the past, when my students shared their firsthand experiences of service, I'd find myself drawn in to the moment, of the chance to see it through their eyes. The dusty air. The heat of the sun as it baked down on them. The sense of fear, of being "on edge" that so many of them described. I'd always been grateful for the stories they shared. It was one thing to understand something intellectually, to hold it at a safe distance. Still, it was another to hear firsthand about the experience of war. Their stories touched me deeply, offering a window into an experience I would never have.

As a social worker I worked with many veterans, many of whom have suffered from PTSD. I often struggled to understand the disconnect between our government's actions and the impact they had on real people. Not just in our country, but in countries all around the world. Now, as I listened to Kwang relay his own experiences to me, those feelings bubbled up inside me. Actions had consequences. To Kwang. To his family.

To the people of South Korea. I felt protective of him. Even though we'd just met, I didn't want him to suffer. He'd seen more in his short life than I had, that was for certain.

In 2011, I took a group of high school students on a service trip to El Salvador. As part of a cultural exchange, we'd gone to visit the former home of Archbishop Oscar Romero, the priest who had been assassinated by an El Salvadoran death squad during the country's civil war. Romero was murdered while he offered Mass, killed by a sniper's bullet as he stood on the altar before the congregants. The Archbishop had been a strong voice in opposition to the government, calling on them to stop the repression and killing of the people of El Salvador. The assassination itself happened in 1980, when I was still a student at Boston College.

Romero's San Salvador home was turned into a museum with artifacts from that time. On display were the vestments he wore on that fateful day, the garments still stained in the Archbishop's blood. We visited the church where the assassination took place and stood on the altar where he preached. Although I knew the history, looking at the bloody vestments and standing on the place where he spoke his final words gave me a deeper appreciation for a moment I'd only read about. As I looked out the door to the opening from where the gunman fired, it allowed me to step into that experience, to understand it in a way that had not been possible before.

And then, the following year, on another service trip, to Nicaragua this time, I came a step closer. I met a Salvadoran man who had been a seminarian under Archbishop Romero. This man was there during that period of turmoil. Had sat at the knee of this peacemaker, this voice for justice. Had been involved in the funeral of this holy man. He was there when the government's troops opened fire on the crowd, amid the pandemonium and bloodshed. One night, as we gathered the students to debrief from the day's activities, he offered a first-hand account of those momentous days. As his gentle voice filled the air, the room became eerily silent.

Hearing his story, seeing the living remnants of a civil war allowed me to travel back in time; to gain a deeper understanding of an experience that I'd only seen from a distance. This too, was true in that moment with Kwang. The idea that this kind and gentle man, barely 20 years old, stood on the front lines defending his country shook me to my core. That he was in such danger, in part because of the actions of the country I called home, made me feel sick to my stomach. How had we become so removed from the human impact of our actions? So disconnected from our humanity? Again, in that moment, as I had in El Salvador and Nicaragua, I felt my heart fill with gratitude for the opportunity to experience something through his eyes, and as we walked this beautiful landscape together, I was struck by the gift he'd given me, the chance to see things as he sees them, to stand, if only for minute, in his shoes.

Kwang and I stopped at a small sandwich shop in Navarrete for lunch. A couple of Frenchmen I'd seen earlier in the day were there and just getting ready to leave. We said hello and then dropped our bags and went inside. I ordered a café con leche and a slice of tortilla and then went out to the table to wait for Kwang. He returned a few minutes later with a freshly made bocadillo de jamón and a large glass of jugo de naranja (orange juice).

He seemed shy, his speech slow and deliberate, his answers to my questions thoughtful. Our conversation was stilted, the way it often is when you're speaking to someone who is not a native speaker. Kwang still lived with his mother and father. He was the eldest in his family and he had younger siblings. He struck me as independent, having traveled so far away from home to undertake this pilgrimage at such a young age. He told me that he was walking the Camino with his parents' blessing, and because he was so young and so far away from home, I was surprised to learn that he had not had much contact with them since he began. In the fall he would begin his studies at the university.

Over the next few weeks, as we make our way to Santiago, I will see him from time to time along the path. We will even share a few more meals together. He will always be alone, yet he each time he welcomes me with a warm smile and we spend a few minutes chatting before one or the other of us makes our way onward.

On the Camino it does not matter where we come from. What language we speak. How old we are or how much money we have. There is no attempt to compete with one another, to leave anyone behind. While people are at odds with each other around the world, the Camino is a respite from the noise that so often divides us. We sleep in simple lodging. We eat common meals. We have left behind the things that separate us. On the Camino we are all the same.

Each day I listened to the stories of the people I met. Each one different. Every person unique. One man began walking from his home in Belgium. Another just lost her husband to cancer. Smitha was a writer from Bangalore, India. Peggy, a young woman from Hong Kong. Raphael a flight attendant from Sao Paulo, Brazil. There were retired professors, students, dentists and healers.

When my children were small, I read them the Margery Williams' story, The Velveteen Rabbit. I'd always loved the story of the toy rabbit who longed to be real. "'Real isn't how you are made,' the skin horse explains to the rabbit. 'It's a thing that happens to you. When a child loves you for a long, long time, not just to play with, but REALLY loves you, then you become Real.'"

Before I met Kwang, South Korea was just a place on a map, but now it is Kwang's home, the place where he and his family live. He has given me a window through which to see, to know and begin to understand. In knowing I can no longer accept actions that will jeopardize his safety or the safety of the people he loves. Although we have lived different lives, value different things and speak different languages, my heart opened a little wider. Kwang is now a part of me. In hearing his story, like the Velveteen Rabbit, Kwang and the people in the place he called home, became real to me.

That afternoon after we left the café, we stopped to look at a mural painted on the side wall of an overpass. It was a silhouette of pilgrims as they passed. The modern mural was a kaleidoscope of colors, like the people on the Camino itself. With the sun behind us, our shadows stretched over the top of the mural, as if we too are part of the painting. We are complicated individuals. We are mothers and fathers. Sisters and brothers. Grandparents, grandchildren and friends. We love and are loved. We work. We play. We cook and we eat together. As the spiritual teacher Ram Dass said, "We're all just walking each other home." Putting one foot in front of the other. Doing the best we can.

That night, as we gathered for dinner, I felt an urgency to share Kwang's story with Debbie and Pat. I was anxious to tell them what I'd learned. I wanted to allow them to see him as I had. As he had done with me, I wanted to make him real.

Day 9 & 10
Nájera to Belorado
Kilometer 192.6

CHAPTER 7

Irish Blessings

The road from Nájera to Santo Domingo de la Calzada wound through lush green rioja vineyards and fields of golden wheat that danced in the gentle breezes of a June summer day. Despite the lack of shade, the path was easy enough to walk and the road stretched on as far as the eye could see. As I charged ahead, planting my walking sticks and finding a rhythm, I came upon Patrick, Maria's older brother. I hadn't seen him since the night we'd all gathered together in the café in Estella four days before.

Despite the heat of the summer sun, Patrick was covered from head to toe, a light blue tee shirt over a long undershirt, a pair of blue pants and a tan bucket hat that covered his balding head. He carried a large pack that listed to one side. He was tall and lean with a thick white mustache and stubbly grey beard.

"Buen Camino," I said as I approached him.

"Buen Camino. How are you doing today?"

"I'm great," I said. "How about you?"

"I'm doing OK. My hip's bothering me a little bit, but I'll be OK."

"Your hip?"

"Yeah, I had hip surgery a while back. Hey, can I ask you a favor? Would you walk on the other side of me? I have a little trouble hearing on that side."

"Of course," I said, and swung around to Patrick's better side.

"Are you the one from Penngrove?" he asked, recalling our introductory conversation from a few nights before. "I used to teach at Wilson School, and then at Penngrove Elementary too. I loved teaching. I miss those kids something fierce."

I'd been shocked the night we first met when his sister, Maria, had introduced herself, mentioning she lived in Rohnert Park. "You're kidding me," I'd said. "That's literally five minutes from where I live." I shook my head in disbelief. Here we were, sharing a table together in a random town thousands of miles from home. The coincidence was extraordinary.

Wilson Elementary School, where Patrick taught, was in Petaluma, the next town over from where I lived. It was one of a number of elementary schools in the local school district. Petaluma was where we'd raised our kids. In fact, my husband had spent a number of years working for the local school district. I wondered if Patrick had ever met him.

"His name doesn't sound familiar, but I retired a number of years ago. I live in Florida now, but I still miss Sonoma County."

I understood. I lived in the northern California wine country. Known for its bountiful vineyards, rolling hills, redwood forests and rugged wild coastline, it is a beautiful place to live. Over the years it had become a tourist destination, with people coming from all around the world to explore the great outdoors and enjoy the extraordinary foods and wines of the region.

As we walked together, I learned that Patrick was an avid hiker. He'd walked sections of both the Pacific Crest Trail on the west coast and the Appalachian Trail on the east. In fact, he told me he'd married his second wife on the Appalachian Trail. This was, however, his first time in Europe and at 73, he was experiencing many things for the first time. Patrick had a gentle soul and playful curiosity about him. In the evening we'd take turns prompting him to try all sorts of things. He'd listen earnestly to whatever pitch he was being given and then without fail he'd inevitably say yes, his eyes twinkling with excitement. According to his sister, he'd never been much of a coffee drinker, but on the Camino he looked forward to his daily café con leche. He could often be seen with a mug of Estrella, the local cerveza. That is, until he tried Sangria, Spain's sweet concoction of ripe fruit and red wine, which turned out to be one of his favorites.

How unpredictable life was. At 73, Patrick was the age my father was when he'd died almost 12 years before from ALS. And yet, here he was, far away from home for the first time in his life, walking 500 miles with his younger sister. It took courage to do what he was doing, and I was enchanted by his adventurous spirit.

In Santo Domingo de la Calzada I made reservations for dinner at Pizzeria La Strada, an Italian restaurant on the Avenida Juan Carlos. We were a big group, so they stuck us in a corner of the back dining room where our raucous laughter wouldn't disturb the other diners. I loved those family dinners. Conor and Emma usually held court, having us all in stitches before too long.

Conor was a bit of enigma. He had an imposing presence, a shaved head and a long, muscular face. His tattooed arms stretched the sleeves of his shirt to their limits. It was rare to see him without his dark sunglasses that seemed to serve as shelter and add to his mysterious charisma. Like Emma, Conor's wit was caustic. "Isn't that grand," he liked to say, punctuating whatever story that had just been shared. 'Grand", I came to learn, was Irish slang that could mean any number of things. "Grand can be wonderful, fine or pure shite," Conor explained. "It really is up to the person listening to figure out."

Despite his tough exterior, there was a softer side to him, a side that was less obvious at first glance. Inside that hardened shell was a depth of emotion, a gentility that he chose to share in words. For years he'd been writing and publishing his poetry. It was that that drew me to him in the first place. Conor was a writer, a poet in the long tradition of Irish poets.

After copious plates of pasta and pizza, several bottles of rioja and glasses of beer, we stumbled back to our albergue full and happy. As I readied myself for bed, I received a text from Emma. "Conor's best friend passed away," it said. It had been an apparent suicide. They would walk tomorrow and then head home to Ireland, cutting their Camino short. "Don't say anything," Emma said as she followed up, "I'm sure he'll tell everyone. He just needs a little time."

The following day I walked alone, my heart heavy as I held Conor's secret. Life's moments were so fleeting. So much could change in the blink of an eye. At the same time, what a strange synchronicity it had. The night before, as I sat across from him at the restaurant, Conor and I debated the value of therapy.

"It's just not something we do," he'd said.

"What?"

"Talk about our feelings."

Of course not, I thought to myself. He's Irish.

I knew from my early family therapy training that we were all socialized to deal with things differently. That family dynamics, life experiences and cultural background set the rules by which we communicate, about what and with whom. In the Italian family I'd grown up in, there were two hard and fast rules when it came to what we shared. The first was that *what happened in the family stayed in the family*. Like an impenetrable brick wall, there was a firm boundary around our family. If there was trouble within, it could not be shared. There was no airing of dirty laundry. No telling tales out of school. We had a reputation to uphold. My father was a local politician and because of that, we were anything but anonymous. Out in the community, people recognized us. Whether it be at school, our after school jobs or while out in the neighborhood, my siblings and I were expected to be on our best behavior. We were the representatives of our parents, they were quick to remind us. There was no mistake about the responsibility we carried out into the world.

But that wasn't the hardest part. The second rule of our family was that *you didn't talk about difficult feelings*, particularly if it had the potential to hurt someone in the family. "If you can't say something nice," my father was fond of telling us, "Don't say anything at all,". We were encouraged, or rather expected, to share feelings of gratitude, appreciation and joy. But disappointment, frustration, or anger? Those were another matter, especially if it had to do with our parents. No, there was no place for that in our family.

But the rules only applied to my siblings and me. Our parents were free to say whatever they wanted, even when it hurt us deeply. As a child I learned to swallow my feelings. Buried deep inside, they became toxic, an emotional cancer that poisoned my relationships with some of the people I loved the most. Sometimes I even took them out on myself.

Now mind you, I didn't know that this was a problem. It was just the way it was. It took me years to unlearn those lessons. My choice to become a social worker, someone who specialized in family therapy, had not been accidental. I witnessed the pain my clients experienced when they did not speak their truth. Not only did it infect their family relationships, but it was at the core of things like alcoholism, drug addiction, depression and even suicide. I'd spent the whole of my career helping people break down the barriers that kept them from speaking honestly to the people they loved. It wasn't their feelings that they should fear. It was what happened when you tried to run from them. The only way to healing was straight through the middle. Feelings were meant to be shared. I knew that with every bone in my body. Perhaps that's why Emma texted me, why she'd told me what was going on with Conor. She was worried about him and she knew I would understand.

The albergue A. Santiago in the town of Belorado was in the middle of nowhere. I found Conor and Emma sitting with a few of the others at a picnic table just outside the albergue's restaurant. Although Conor's eyes were shaded behind his extra dark sunglasses, I could still see the pain in his tear-stained face and my heart ached for him. As I approached the table, I wondered if he'd said anything to the others but as I set down my beer and found a seat, I quickly realized that he had. We made plans to have dinner, our last one together. Conor and Emma would head back to Ireland in the morning. I went off to take a shower and get some laundry done.

I got to the dining room early, hoping to find a few minutes to talk to Conor alone. I found him sitting at the bar, sunglasses still in place, his hands wrapped around a tall pint of beer.

The room was empty, but for the two of us. I put my hand on his shoulder as I came up behind him.

"I'm so sorry about your friend," I said. "Is there anything I can do?" I hoped he would feel comfortable enough to confide in me.

He forced a smile. "Thanks. It's such a shock," he said. "Johnny was my best mate. The best man at Emma and my wedding."

I stood silently beside him, my arm still resting on his shoulder. The room felt heavy around us and for a moment everything seemed to slow down. I was struck by how different he was in that moment. The tough exterior no longer seemed as daunting. His pale Irish complexion betrayed by the redness of his tears. Until then he'd been a bit of mystery to me. I found him guarded, as if he didn't want you getting too close. But now, with this unplanned event there'd been a shift in him, a vulnerability he'd not shown before. I felt a deeper connection with him. I wondered if he felt it too.

Conor's sadness permeated the room. Soon the door opened and I looked up to see Irish English John coming toward us. John bought himself a beer, one for me and another for Conor. It was what we did on the Camino. After we took our shower, put on clean clothes and did our laundry, we'd gather before dinner over frosty mugs of cerveza or clara, beer mixed with lemon soda. I looked forward to those evening celebrations, but this one was different. I was worried about Conor. About how, in that moment, a stiff pint could be a temptation to numb his pain. I knew he didn't want to be a burden on us but I hoped he would allow himself to feel. Still, there wasn't much I could do in the moment. I lifted my pint with the others and we toasted Conor's mate.

That night, as we sat around the dinner, the mood ping-ponged between playful and somber. We carried on, sharing stories and laughs and although I joined in, I found myself sneaking a peak at Conor every now and then. I was consumed with his pain, with the desire to do something to lessen it if I could, but at the same time I knew that it was his to carry. At some point Maria raised her glass. "To Conor and Emma. May the road rise up to meet you. May the wind be always at your back. May the sun shine warm upon your face; the rains fall soft upon your fields and until we meet again, may God hold you in the palm of His hand." We joined her and lifted our glasses into the air. "And to Johnny," she added.

"To Johnny," we repeated in unison. Tears streamed down my face.

After dinner we talked and laughed like old friends who'd known each other far longer than the few days we'd been together. Emma taught Patrick how to Irish dance and Patrick returned the favor by teaching her to two-step. At 73, he still could move. Conor gave Patrick a small Irish flag with instructions to find a suitable place to plant it somewhere along the way in memory of Johnny. "You'll know where," he'd said. And then, before we realized, it was time to say goodbye.

As I waited my turn, I thought back to that night in Estella. It seemed so long ago. In just a little over a week, so much had happened. Like the mountains we'd climbed that first day, my heart filled with an overwhelming joy. Still, as I faced saying goodbye, the sadness seemed unbearable. Saying goodbye had never been easy for me. We'd only known each other for a little more than a week, but in that time, we'd become family.

Tears poured down my face as I hugged Emma goodbye.

"Oh no you don't," she said, her Irish brogue making the words dance as they fell from her lips, but when I looked up, she was crying too. "We'll see each other again. You're not getting rid of us that easily."

I hoped she was right.

Journal Entry

Day 11 - Belorado to Agés

27.7 kilometers (18 miles) An early morning start for a long walk today. The 6 a.m. departure without coffee was not my favorite. I walked alone most of the day through rolling hills of wheat and the Oca forest. There were a number of beautiful murals today painted on the sides of buildings.

I ate a picnic lunch in a pilgrim's grove with the Irish docs amidst wildly painted trees and carved wooden sculptures. They are so much fun. We are beginning to see storks nesting in the bell towers.

I am finding that I actually like walking alone. Surprising. My mind wanders – but it does not settle on much except a profound sense of gratitude.

It was cold and windy today, a far cry from the extreme heat we've had so far.

Day 12 - Ages to Burgos

22.3 kilometers (13.9 miles) The road to Burgos. Cold wind. A steep climb and a long slow walk into a busy city.

The Burgos cathedral was amazing – a massive Gothic structure with spires that reached high into the sky. I met a teacher from ASU who had a large group of service learning students who'd just finished a semester long course that culminated in an international service commitment. The students were working in collaboration with an elementary school in Burgos. It sounded like an amazing program.

We saw the tiny coffin of El Cid, although we found out that his body is actually buried in the cathedral in León. Debbie, Pat and I stayed in a private room with our very own bath. The walk from Ages was so windy and cold that we had to turn on the heat to get warm!

I had the best pilgrim meal so far... Garlic sauteed calamari and soup at a local restaurant next door to the hostal with Irish English John and Jason from Australia.

Day 13 - Burgos to Hontanas

31.4 kilometers (19.5 miles) Took one last look at the cathedral before the long walk out of Burgos today and then onto the meseta. Fields of wheat. Piles of rocks and a bright blue sky. More churches and flowers. Feeling so much gratitude.

We arrived in Hontanas, a beautiful old village and checked into our albergue – an 18ᵗʰ century building – a wonderful triple room. After a shower and a rest I went out to the street and had a beer with Irish English John and Jason. The sun was shining, the church bells were ringing – pilgrims crowded into the square all drinking and talking... These are the wonderful moments of the Camino experience.

A shared meal – a shared laugh – it is these moments when I want to pinch myself – it's such an amazing experience, even with the hard days of walking, the sore feet – it can be difficult but at the end of the day it's all worth it.

It's hard to believe we have been walking for 13 days. We are under 500 K from Santiago. As difficult as it has been, it has gone so quickly.

DAY 14
HONTANAS, KILOMETER
317.7

CHAPTER 8

Bearing Witness

The alarm went off at 5:45. I rubbed my eyes and stretched out my legs but seconds later the cramps that had become customary the past few mornings returned and I reached down to knead the knots that bulged from my calves. I have been on the Camino for two weeks. Today, the goal is to make Boadilla del Camino, 28.5 kilometers (17.7 miles) away. I dress quickly, splash water on my face, brush my teeth and head out to find a café con leche with Debbie and Pat before we begin to walk.

At breakfast I share the text I received that morning from my husband. It's a picture of Rusty, my beautiful 11 year-old rescue dog. He is bathed in sunshine, his golden fur covered in the morning light. "We miss you," the text said. "We're rooting for you. Go get 'em." Pat notes that there is a steep hill today, just on the other side of Castrojeriz. This has become a ritual, his daily scouting report. Each morning, before we begin, Pat reads the guidebook and reviews the maps in preparation for the day. "Today will be an easy one," he promises, "Except for the one hill, we should be pretty flat." I laugh. Hills, no hills, rain, or shine, it doesn't matter. We're going to walk anyway.

On the way out of Hontanas, I draw their attention to a crude stone figure of a man peeing. It reminds me of the Mannekin Pis, an infamous sculpture I saw in Brussels many years ago. Boughs of pink roses form a heart against a stone wall. Although we set out together, before long I am well ahead of them, the dirt road stretched out before me. Morning has become my favorite time to walk, when the air is cool, the sun still low in the sky. The day before me unblemished and ripe with possibility.

Walking along the sparsely populated dirt road, I quickly find my rhythm. With the sun at my back, I pause to snap a picture of my elongated shadow. The Camino is an exercise in sensory awareness. The warmth of the midday sun. The crunch of footsteps. The whirr of the occasional bicycles that pass by. This morning, like the others, I am swept up in the sound of birds, a chorus of complex harmonies that rings in my ears. I hear what I think is a cuckoo. I look around hoping to confirm my suspicions with someone else, but I am alone. I smile. It feels as though I have stumbled on something special, like finding a four-leaf clover. Do the birds sound like this at home, I wonder? Am I too distracted to notice?

A few miles from town I stumble upon the ruins of the monastery of San Antón. I step through the arch that spreads across the path and again I am overcome with a sense of wonder. As I explore what remains of this ancient site, poking my head into the nooks and crannies that have survived, I sense an energy that I cannot articulate. I peek through an archway inside what might have been the nave of the old church to see a group of pilgrims standing together, a small table and a few chairs. I later learn that there is an albergue inside. I wish I had known. It would have been a magical place to stay.

The road rolls out in front of me to uncover a landscape reminiscent of a Cezanne print that hung on my office wall many years ago. Acres of greens and yellows. Trees dotting the earth. A field of wheat. The sunlight and clouds play tricks on my eyes. The greens deepen. The wheat turns from yellow to a golden brown. I pass a field of poppies and smile as I think about a scene from "The Wizard of Oz", a favorite film from my childhood. "Poppies," the voice of the Wicked Witch of the West rings in my ears, "Poppies will make her sleep." There are poppies everywhere.

The poppies trigger a rush of memories. I am young, maybe 10 years old or so. It is Easter Sunday and we are visiting my grandparents Maggio, my father's mother and father. We have already eaten dinner and my mother instructs us to put on our pajamas before we gather around the television to watch the annual showing of "The Wizard of Oz". I am wearing a long flannel nightgown as my brothers, sister and I settle in on the couch, tucked under a few of my grandmother's crocheted blankets as we get ready to watch. Later, when the movie has finished, we will lie down in the back of the wood paneled Country Squire station wagon and make the hour-long journey home. My mind begins to drift. Memories of my grandmother flood my thoughts and I begin to cry.

I feel her presence as I walk. I hear her voice in my ears. She has been gone for many years and I am surprised that she has come to me in this moment. A series of memories run through my mind. I think about the multistory brownstone she and my grandfather lived in in Brooklyn, New York. We took turns spending weeks in the summer with her, my sister and I and then my brothers. We'd take the bus into Manhattan to go to the Museum of Natural History. We'd eat lunch at the Horn and Hardart, the legendary automat on Broadway. I can still see the rows of glass enclosed cases filled with pies and cakes for the choosing. There is apple and cherry and my favorite, lemon meringue. She was a large woman, tall and broad shouldered, but there was a gracefulness about her, gentle and kind. I missed her.

In Castrojeriz, there is a small museum inside the church. I wander around looking at the beautiful wood carvings, the rose window and the enormous gold retablo that sits behind the altar. The stained glass is a favorite of mine, the light streaming through the panes and casting a warm glow on the stone floors below. As I am about to leave I run into Smitha, the woman from Bangalore, India. A friend has told her that there are skulls carved into the walls of the church, but she cannot find them. I join her for a few minutes to look. We stand outside the church, scanning the walls, but there are no skulls to be found. I wave goodbye to her and carry on, but a few minutes later, there they are. On the outside of a different church. I smile as I pass by. I hope that Smitha will see them.

Outside of Castrojeriz, the long steep hill that Pat has warned us about awaits. Filled with a quiet determination, I put my head down and begin to climb. By now I have learned to use my poles as I walk. I stretch them out in front of me, planting them into the ground as I pull myself towards them.

They are an extension of my person. I am one with my poles. I climb and climb. A quick pace. My climbing pace. I stride past a gentleman resting along the side of the path. He is older, with gray hair, of average height and a trim build. European, I guess. "Buen Camino," I say.

"Buen Camino. Poco a poco," he laughs, patting his hand into the air, cautioning me to slow down.

I smile, lowering my head and resume planting my poles into the dirt as I continue my climb. I am breathing heavily. The sun is hot and there is no shade on this section of the route. Sweat pours down my face. I wipe my brow mid-stride and continue on. I will not allow myself to stop until I reach the top.

At the crest of the hill I take off my pack and give myself a few minutes to catch my breath while my heart rate returns to normal. I sip some water and look back to trace the path I have just taken. The road descends into the valley, hugging the hillside and winding its way through a myriad of multi-colored fields, finally disappearing into the horizon. Reaching the crest of the climb is the man who'd teased me on the way. He smiles as he comes towards me. I smile back.

"Well done," I say, giving him a "thumbs up" as he makes his way to the top. He pauses and takes a long drink of water. He too, is breathing heavily.

"Buen Camino," he says as he approaches me.

"Hard," I say, clenching my fists and offering a pantomime to make sure he understands.

"Yes. You go very fast," he says.

I respond with a smile. "Where are you from?" I ask. I cannot place his accent.

"France," he says. "And you?"

"The United States," I say.

"Ah, American."

I nod. I lift my pack and slide my arms through the straps, slipping it back over my shoulders. "Have a good walk," I say.

Buen Camino," he says. "You must take your time,"

I laugh. This is just the way I do it. I just keep going. I am nothing if not determined.

"OK," I say, "Buen Camino." And I am off again.

People leapfrog all day along the Camino. A string of pilgrims walks by. An hour later you might pass them. I see the Frenchman several times in the days to come. Each time he greets me warmly, as if he is meeting an old friend. "Buen Camino," he smiles. He calls me 'the climber'. We walk together for a while. I learn that he is from Alsace. That this is his first Camino. Despite his teasing of me, he too walks quickly. While he is walking the first part alone, his wife will join him in León. He is worried about that, unsure if she will be able to keep up. Despite spending time together, I never learn his name. Like him, there are many others. Faces that become familiar along The Way, whose names I will never know.

And yet. And yet.

Buen Camino. Two simple words. On a typical day I will repeat those words dozens and dozens of times. "Buen Camino," you say to everyone you pass. "Buen Camino," they reply. "Buen Camino," the townspeople say as you walk by. "Buen Camino," says the man in the café as he hands you your change. The greeting is always the same. Buen Camino. A wish for a good journey. In the early days of walking it felt awkward, a greeting that had not yet earned its purpose. But now to say it is as routine as breathing. Today, as I walked, something else became clear to me. "Buen Camino" is not just a wish, it is also an acknowledgement, a way of bearing witness. A way to say, "*I see you.*"

As I walk I let this thought settle in my brain. I begin to think about what it means to see and be seen. It seems so simple, but I know it is not. I race to class rushing past students in the hallway. I push a cart through the grocery store, rarely making eye contact with the people around me. We are busy. Preoccupied. Worried about what comes next. We race from here to there. Did the birds sing at home, I'd wondered? I had to confess, I did not know. How difficult it was to notice.

A number of years ago I was working as the clinical director of a homeless shelter. One of the residents, a man named Jamie, was about to leave the shelter for permanent housing. As part of his preparations to leave, he was making the rounds saying goodbye to the residents and staff, thanking them for supporting him along the way.

Jamie was in his 40s. The son of a single mother, he never knew his birth father. As was the case with many in our population, he'd struggled most of his life. Fractured by poverty, homelessness and addiction, his family was no safe haven. Tall and handsome with chocolate brown skin and deep soulful eyes, he had been raised by his grandmother, a woman he loved deeply. As a young man he ended up on the streets and struggled with mental illness and a drug addiction of his own. Now an adult, he'd bounced from place to place, sleeping in his car, a friend's couch and even outdoors, wherever he could find room. His addiction to drugs landed him in prison for a period of time. When I met him, he'd just been released and with nowhere to go, he'd found his way to the shelter. After a number of months in our program, he regained his sobriety and stabilized his mental health.

That day, as he prepared to leave, he made his way around the room, handing out hugs and shaking hands. This man was a different man than the one I'd met many months before. Hardened by the pain he'd experienced, he'd cloaked himself in a coat of armor, a defense that worked well to protect him but also served to keep others away.

He'd let me peek beneath his shell when he joined a writing group I was leading for the residents. I watched as he carefully penned both poetry and prose. Our group of rag tag writers hung on his every word as he read us his stories of growing up with his grandmother from whom he'd developed a love of gardening. Inside the room, with pen in hand, he allowed us to see a different side of himself, a humanity that hid deep beneath his hardened shell.

"I want to thank you," he said as he made his way to me.

"You're welcome," I said. "For what?"

"I don't know if you remember, but the first time I met you, you reached out and shook my hand."

"Yes," I said, confused.

"Most people don't even look at us," he said. "They look past us, as if we aren't even there. You looked me straight in the eye. I will never forget that."

We don't always know the impact the simple act of noticing has on others, but we know when it is missing. As a child, it was the thing I wanted most. To be seen by my parents. I wanted them to recognize my struggles. To understand my pain. As a young woman I still longed for my mother to see me, to accept me for who I was, not the person she wanted me to be. But all she could see was her own reflection. An image constructed from her own wants and needs, not those of her daughter. I felt alone, vulnerable, a wounded vessel torn open and waiting for someone to notice.

I carried those wants into adulthood, not fully under-standing why. The desire to be truly seen by those I loved the most. By my siblings. My husband. My children and even my friends. In social work I found a career that allowed me to do for others what I'd wanted to be done for me, to bear witness to the efforts of ordinary life, to be present when my clients struggled, to share their burdens and revel in their successes. Social work was an opportunity to walk beside others in the journey of life. It had always felt like a privilege, to be allowed to witness someone else's journey. To hear their story. To be allowed in.

There were no strangers on The Camino de Santiago de Compostela. They were, as the Irish poet William Butler Yeats is believed to have said, "only friends you haven't met yet." With each "Buen Camino" came an opening, an acknowledgement of a person, a journey, a struggle. It was a gift I'd received just that morning, from the Frenchman from Alsace. "Buen Camino," he'd said to me as I passed him on the way. *I see you.* Just one fast walker bearing witness to another.

And so it was with Peggy, a young woman from Hong Kong I met two days later on the road to Terradillos de los Templarios.

I was sitting on a picnic table in the only shade anywhere to be found. It was midday and the sunbaked Via Aquitana, the dry Roman road, was already beginning to chew up my feet. I pulled off my shoes and socks, wiggling my toes to give them room to breathe. A new blister was forming on the back of my right heel and another on the ball of the same foot. This stretch of road was a long one. There'd been nowhere to stop to get water. No small café to grab a glass of freshly squeezed orange juice. Just this small cluster of picnic tables in the only section of shade for miles.

I saw Peggy coming. I did not know her name at the time but I recognized her wide brimmed hat and lavender shirt. I'd seen her several times over the past few days. She walked slowly. Methodically. Firmly planting her poles into the ground. Often, she was alone. I'd said hello and "Buen Camino" each time I'd passed her, but we hadn't had a chance to go farther than that. Now, as she approached, something was wrong. I could see it. Her stride was labored and she seemed to be in pain.

"How are you doing?" I asked as she came over to where I was sitting. Her eyes filled with tears. "What's wrong?"

"My knee," she said, her limited English failing her in that exact moment.

"Here, sit down. Which knee is it? Do you have any Advil?" I asked. "Something for the pain?" Without waiting for her to answer, I opened up my backpack and fished out my medicine bag. I handed her some Advil and a couple of tissues.

"Thank you," she said, wiping away her tears.

"Do you have something to wrap it?" I asked, but realized she didn't understand. I pulled out my ace bandage, the one I'd bought at the café vending machine on the third day when I'd twisted my ankle on the descent from Alto de Perdón, and pantomimed a wrapping motion around my knee.

She looked puzzled. "Here," I said. "Let me help you." I tapped the seat of the picnic table, encouraging her to rest her leg there so I could get the leverage I needed to wrap it up. "OK?"

She nodded. She was wearing a pair of black leggings, tight against her skin. I strapped the bandage to the outside, wrapping it firmly around and around and fastening it with a safety pin. "This should help," I said.

By now a few other pilgrims had gathered, wondering how they could help. Someone suggested calling a cab, perhaps she could get a ride to the next town where she might spend the night. Peggy sat on the picnic table for a while, taking a few sips of water as she took the pills I'd given her. She was still crying, still wiping away the tears as she waited for the Advil to kick in.

After a while I decided it was time to get going. I checked in with Peggy to see if there was anything else I could do to help. I hoped she was going to be OK. She seemed to be in a great deal of pain. She waved me off. "I'll be OK," she said. I hesitated for a minute or two, and then pulled on my pack and got back on the road. I thought about Peggy as I walked, half expecting to see a taxicab coming up behind me.

By midafternoon, I'd arrived at the albergue with Irish English John who'd caught up with me soon after I left Peggy. I took a shower, washed my clothes and hung them out to dry before I set out to have a cerveza con limón and a snack of potato chips. I pulled up a seat at one of a handful of café tables on the large lawn in front of the albergue.

I could see the road from where I sat. As I watched for Debbie and Pat, Peggy's familiar wide brimmed hat and lavender shirt came into view. "Peggy," I yelled. "Peggy! You made it."

I was so happy to see her, so relieved to see that she was still walking. I'd felt so badly leaving her at the picnic table, worried that she wouldn't be able to continue, but I wasn't sure what else I could do. I'd been thinking about her ever since. I'd even told Irish English John about her. Still, there she was. I waited for her to come through the gate.

But as she approached the gate, she continued on, past the gate and down the path. She hadn't heard me. I might have gone after her had I been able to move, but my feet were throbbing and before long she was out of eyesight, disappearing into a sea of other peregrinos. I looked away, feeling sheepish and a little sad. I wanted her to see me. I wanted to know how she was doing. I wondered if I would ever see her again.

A few minutes later, Irish English John showed up, beer in hand and sat down beside me. I pushed the bag of potato chips his way.

DAY 16
CARRIÓN DE LOS CONDES
KILOMETER 370.7

CHAPTER 9

Simple Gifts

Bodies packed the foyer of the Albergue Parroquial de Santa Maria del Camino. Beneath a short winding staircase that led to the dormitory rooms, peregrinos squeezed onto a wooden bench that wrapped around the room, their shoulders touching one another like sardines in a small tin can. When there was no more room on the bench, people began to fill the stairs and floor, using every nook and cranny of what normally served as the entrance to this municipal lodging.

It had been the kind of day where unexplained tears hovered just below the surface. I'd walked alone in the morning but by midday, as he did most days, Irish English John caught up with me. We arrived in Carrión de los Condes by midafternoon. Debbie, Pat and I were sharing a room in a lovely albergue with real bed linen and fresh towels. We'd already taken our showers and gone off in different directions to explore the town.

Many of the towns along the Camino were more nondescript villages than full-fledged towns and the truth was, I had a hard time distinguishing one from the other. Small stucco buildings that opened onto tiny squares. A café here and there. The sun faded awning of a tiny mercado. But Carrión de los Condes was different. Carrión de los Condes had the singing nuns.

Except for the brief mention in the guidebook I was using, I'd likely not have even known about this town's unusual feature. The details were sketchy. Where, when and what they would sing was a complete mystery. But since I'd first read about them in the guidebook, I knew I had to see them.

I asked the owner of the albergue if he knew where I might find the sisters. He looked at me quizzically,, and then directed me across the street to the cathedral. But it was midday, the time of the traditional Spanish siesta, and the doors to the cathedral were locked. Assuming it would open later in the afternoon, I opted to walk around town while I waited. In the small grassy square just outside the cathedral, Marc and Martina were eating ice cream. Martina was a tall and slender Croat, with brown eyes and long brown hair. We'd met early on the Camino when we'd shared a room in a wonderful albergue in Zubiri. Marc was a lanky Aussie with blonde hair, a slightly greying goatee and a big broad smile. Martina and Marc were often together.

One day as I was walking along, I heard singing. *"O Suzanna, oh don't you cry for me, for I come from Alabama with a banjo on my knee.*" I turned to find the two of them coming up behind me, singing at the top of their lungs. I laughed. It was an unexpected sight, a Croat and an Aussie singing songs of old Americana, let alone a song that called specifically to me. I joined in.

"Do you know Waltzing Mathilda?" I asked Marc. It was the only Australian song I knew.

"You know Waltzing Mathilda?" he asked, surprised.

"Waltzing Mathilda, Waltzing Mathilda, You'll come a waltzing Mathilda with me," I sang, "My father used to sing it all the time."

Marc's face broke out into a wide grin. An activity director for a senior care facility, he was playful and creative, a truly joyful soul. I asked them if they knew anything about the nuns. "We heard they'd be singing at the municipal albergue at 6:00," he said. I thanked them and told them I'd meet them there.

By now the large wooden doors to the cathedral were propped open. When I stepped inside, I breathed in the instant coolness of the huge stone structure, a welcome break from the heat of the late afternoon. Like so many of the local cathedrals, this one was fairly simple except for a spectacular gold altarpiece that filled the apse. As I found my way up to the front of the church, I heard singing. A group of sisters clad in white habits stood in the front pew, accompanied by one of their own on an electric piano. Over their habits, the sisters wore white fleece jackets, the kind most often worn by outdoor enthusiasts and sport fans. I chuckled to myself. Once, when I was in high school, I was stunned to see Sister Anthony, our Chemistry nun, wearing pajamas on the annual retreat. It was the first time I'd understood that nuns were people, too.

Their soprano voices were dwarfed by the expansive space. For a moment I wondered if this was what I was looking for. Perhaps Marc and Martina were wrong. And yet the church was almost empty except for a few of us who had stumbled upon this surprise performance. I listened for a few minutes and then quietly found my way out the door.

I arrived at the albergue early enough to find a seat on the bench. As I leaned against the wall my insides felt shaky, like worn wooden slats on a rickety old bridge. It seemed I might cry at any moment. I took one deep breath after another, trying hard to compose myself. Debbie and Pat came in shortly thereafter, as did Marc and Martina, Raphael, the gentle Brazilian and dozens of other peregrinos I did not know. The room was ripe with anticipation as more and more people squeezed in, saying hello to each other with a "Buen Camino" and a smile. Before long the nuns joined us, the same sisters I'd seen at the church. They carried instruments with them. The electric piano from the church was replaced by a couple of guitars, a handful of percussion instruments and a stack of well used song sheets. As they lined up across the front of the room, a quiet descended around us. Now that I was looking directly at them, they were younger than I realized, their soft skin and dark hair peeked out from under their white veils.

"Bienvenidos," the youngest one said. She had a kind face and a warm smile and spoke English fairly well. She couldn't have been much older than 30. "Welcome. Before we get started, we'd like you to introduce yourselves. Tell us where you are from and why you are walking the Camino."

Why are you walking the Camino? It was the question I'd heard most often since I'd begun my journey on the 31st of May. Why *was* I walking the Camino? Despite the fact that I'd been faced with that question more times than I could count, I hadn't settled on an answer. *I was turning 60 this year and it seemed like a good thing to do to celebrate a big birthday. Or, I was walking in remembrance of my mother who'd recently died. Or, in honor if my father who'd died from ALS.* I'd said any number of things when people asked.

Many of the people I met were clear about why they were walking. Adriana, a woman from Sao Paolo, was celebrating her recovery from cancer. Oklahoma and his two sons were carrying his wife's ashes to rest in Santiago. Emma and Conor were raising money for a favorite charity at home. Even Irish English John could say why he was walking. An avid walker, he came so his wife, an ardent tennis fan, could watch the French Open without having to worry about him. Perhaps it wasn't the most altruistic of reasons, but at least he knew why he was here.

But me, I wasn't so sure. I don't know why I felt the need to have a reason. Surely, just wanting to walk the Camino was reason enough, but I felt pulled towards something deeper. To understand what had drawn me to this journey. While all of the answers I could come up with sounded good enough on the surface, none of them felt right. They were parts of an answer, I thought, but not all of it. My parents *were* on my mind most days. On the Camino, pilgrims tie a scallop shell to their pack as a symbol of the journey. Before I left California, I gathered three shells of my own, shells I collected years before from a beach on Sanibel Island on the west coast of Florida. My parents owned a vacation home there and it was a place we'd all loved, where we'd spent time together as a family. They were not the traditional Spanish scallop shells, but they would do the trick. I inscribed my mother and father's name in two of the shells, and then made a third for me. I tied them to my pack with string, talismans to remind me as I walked.

The truth was, I didn't really *know* what had drawn me to the Camino. From the first time I'd heard about the ancient pilgrimage, I knew I had to go. And so here I was, in this municipal albergue in a tiny little town packed full of people I had not yet met, from places I had never heard of, speaking languages I did not understand. That's the way it had been for 15 days.

And then there was my reaction in the moment. My efforts to steady myself were failing. I felt my breath catch in my throat and before long I felt the sting of tears in my eyes. I considered putting on my sunglasses, but I didn't want to draw further attention to myself. The introductions began, beginning with an older Dutch man with silver hair and broad shoulders who sat at the end of the bench.. As I listened to my fellow pilgrims introduce themselves, the struggle to get my emotions under control continued. There were folks from Spain and Poland, Germany and Sweden. It was their first Camino or their fourth. They were walking with their wife or their daughter, their mother or a friend - to celebrate their anniversary, in gratitude for their recovery from back surgery or to deepen their faith.

With each testimony I fought to hold back tears. What would I say? How could I express what I was feeling in that moment? Could I even find the words or would I just dissolve into a pool of emotion as I always seemed to do when I felt overwhelmed. Despite the fact that I'd had more than two weeks to arrive at an answer to this fundamental question, I still did not fully understand. What were my tears about? Why was I so feeling so vulnerable?

As the introductions moved around the room edging ever closer towards me, I could feel the pressure inside me grow. "My name is Suzanne," I said. My voice trembled. "I'm from California, in the United States." I looked straight ahead, to where the sisters were sitting. I could hear my voice crack and I paused for a second to steady myself again. "I'm turning 60 this year and…" I forced a smile as I let my voice trail off. I had managed to avoid a complete breakdown.

Debbie jumped in, picking up where I left off as though she understood I could not continue. "I'm walking with my husband," she said, her voice too, heavy with emotion. Pat had introduced himself in a similar way. They were two peas in the same pod.

"Breathe," I kept telling myself. "Just breathe." I looked down at the song sheet that rested in my lap. It was filled with songs from all around the world. There were songs in English and French, Spanish and German. The lyrics blurred as tears dripped from my eyes.

After the introductions were finished, the sisters led us in song. I hummed along to those I did not know. Eventually we came to the unofficial Camino anthem, Ultreia, believed to be inspired by the Codex Calixtinus, or book of St. James, the first known travel guide of the Camino written in the 12th century. The book was now housed in the cathedral in Santiago. As the sisters sang the Latin verses, the pilgrims joined in at the chorus, *Ultreïa! Ultreïa! E suseia Deus adjuva nos!* Loosely translated, it was a greeting of encouragement in the early days of the pilgrimage. Onward and upward. Keep going until we meet again. Our voices swelled and permeated the room, getting louder and louder with every chorus. The ranges and octaves and various accents created a harmony unlike anything I had ever heard before. I sang through the tears that streamed down my face.

As the others began to leave, I milled around wanting to make a connection with one of the sisters. "Muchismas gracias Hermana," I said, when I made my way to her. *Thank you, Sister.* She reached out to me, touching my arm with her hand. I thought I saw concern in her face and felt the need to explain. "Estoy muy emocional. Esto es un experiencia muy extraordinario para me." It was truly an extraordinary evening.

"De nada," the sister responded as she reached out to give me a hug. "Vaya con Dios, peregrina." *May you go with God.*

An hour later I returned to the cathedral for the pilgrim Mass. It had been more than two weeks since that Mass on the first night at the monastery in Roncesvalles. It was traditional for the priest to offer a prayer for the pilgrims at the end of Mass. In Carrión de los Condes, he invited all of us to the altar. "Buenos tardes," he said. "Quien es de España?" A handful of pilgrims raised their hands. "Buenos dias," the priest replied. "de Italia?" "Buongiorno," he said, greeting a handful more. "Alemania? Francia? China?" He ticked through more than a dozen countries, each time welcoming us in our native language.

"I would like to invite each of you to come forward for a personal blessing," he said in English after he was done. "After you receive your blessing, the sisters have a small gift for you."

"It is very lightweight," one of the sisters added with a smile and we all laughed. Two weeks in we were very mindful about adding any weight to our already overloaded packs.

I got in line behind a young Spaniard I recognized from the earlier gathering with the nuns and folded my hands as if I were going to receive communion. When I reached the front of the line, I bowed my head and closed my eyes as the priest placed his hands on my shoulders and recited a version of the prayer I had heard after the Mass that first night in Roncesvalles.

"O God, who brought your servant Abraham out of the land of the Chaldeans, protecting him in his wanderings, who guided the Hebrew people across the desert, we ask that you watch over us, your servants, as we walk in the love of your name to Santiago de Compostela.
Be for us our companion on the walk,
Our guide at the crossroads, Our breath in our weariness,
Our protection in danger,
Our albergue on the Camino,
Our shade in the heat,
Our light in the darkness,

Our consolation in our discouragements,
And our strength in our intentions.
So that with your guidance we may arrive safe and sound at
the end of the road and enriched with grace and virtue we return
safely to our homes filled with joy.
In the name of Jesus Christ our Lord, Amen.
Apostle Santiago, pray for us.
Santa Maria, pray for us."

"Amen," I said and moved in line to await the gift from the sisters. I reached out my hand to receive a small, two-inch, multicolored paper star.

"This is to remind you that you are the light," she said to us after we had all received our stars. "Like stars in the sky, you are called to bring light into the world. One by one, you can be the light for someone. But remember that you are not alone. Each night the sky is full of stars. And like the stars in the sky, when we join together, we can illuminate even the darkest night."

I turned the small paper star over in my hand and inhaled deeply as if to breathe in the energy of the room in that moment. The sister's words, while spoken to the dozens of us who had gathered felt personal, as if rekindling the spark of something I once knew and now needed to be reminded of. *I see you,* it felt like she was saying. *I see what is in your heart. Your passion for others, your desire to be of service. Your talents. Your wisdom. Your strength. You. Suzanne, you are seen. In the sea of stars, your light shines brightly.*

It was something I'd struggled with my whole life, the desire to be acknowledged and the pull to belong. I had spent my whole adult life toggling between the two spaces. I longed to be understood, to be seen for who I was, and yet I also yearned to belong, to be part of something bigger than myself. A star in a huge sea of stars. I loved the sense of belonging I found in family. In friendships and in work. It was the place I felt most alive. The collective fight to be a force of good in the world.

On the Camino I leaned into the connection to others. The greetings of "Buen Camino." The hours spent chatting as we walked along. The camaraderie I felt when we gathered together at the end of the day. These were my favorite moments of the Camino, these moments of belonging.

I'd grown up in a boisterous Italian family with a mother who dressed us in matching outfits, signed us up for group piano lessons and swimming classes. We would be asked to be loyal to one another, to swear our allegiance to the family and I agreed to do so. Being a part of something was second nature to me. Despite having my own hopes and dreams, the family came first. Loyalty to my family would always come first.

And yet I struggled with the need to differentiate myself from them. I loved being a part of the collective, but I also wanted to be seen for who I was, to distinguish myself from the other stars in my sky. The tug between my two realities was painful. I struggled to find my footing, caught in the undertow of the powerful wave that was my family. At times I chose to step away. I'd abandoned an acceptance to graduate school to study Art History and joined the Jesuit Volunteer Corps, a choice my parents vehemently disapproved of. I'd moved to Montana and then California, far away from my family in New Jersey. I'd married a man very different from me, despite my parents' objections. We'd built a life together. Bought a home and raised two children. To my parents it felt like rejection. To me, a chance to forge my own path.

But there had been crossroads in my journey. How does one know which way to go? At times I felt like Dorothy when she meets the Scarecrow in *The Wizard of Oz*. I had not always made the right choice. Sometimes I'd made choices for the wrong reasons. I recognized that now. Each step had been painful. Many felt disloyal. With each one my heart ached. To be separate while being a part of had not been easy. The in-between was a lonely place to be. I tucked the star into my pocket and stepped out into the evening light.

Over the past two weeks, I'd spent a good part of every day with Debbie and Pat. Although we walked at different speeds, we began each day with a café con leche and then set off together, only to end the day at the same place. Over time we began to book lodging ahead, opting for triple rooms whenever possible. The private rooms were a little more comfortable and saved us from having to stay in the larger dormitory accommodations. If I got to the albergue early, I'd check in and then wait for them to arrive. Over the past few weeks, I'd become accustomed to the routine.

But I hadn't seen Debbie and Pat since I'd left them at the albergue and we hadn't made plans for dinner. Since it was already past the time we usually ate, I imagined they'd probably done so already. I set out to find Irish English John. Still reverberating with the experience at Mass, I didn't want to eat alone. I wandered back towards the albergue, hoping to find my friend along the way. But the streets were quiet and he was nowhere to be found. My heart sank. Maybe I'd just go back to the room.

But I was hungry. Next to the albergue was a restaurant. "The best food in town," the hospitalero said when we'd checked in. I summoned up my courage and pulled open the door. There was Irish English John, staring at me.

"There you are," he said. "I've been looking for you. We're just about to get dinner. Come join us." I wouldn't have to eat alone after all. *Like the stars in the sky, we are not alone. We are never alone.*

CHAPTER 10

Socks

I stretched the sock as wide as I could to pull it over my left heel. The wool fabric stuck to my skin. The two blisters had morphed into one, forming a gross puffy pillow that covered the entire surface. The balls of both feet were raw as well, the result of a multitude of blisters stacked on top of one another. I fell back on the bed and looked up at the ceiling, estimating the number of steps it would take to get to the bathroom. I needed a shower badly but the idea of getting up again was going to take some effort. Thirty minutes later, my sheet drenched in the sweat of another day of walking, I was ready to try. I sat at the edge of the bed and scoped out my next move.

Three days earlier, while walking along the meseta, the wide "plain of Spain" that stretched between Burgos and Astorga, I could feel the familiar sting of a blister's birth. The sun beat down on the dry earth as I walked alone and I learned soon enough what had been the reputation of this particular stretch of the Camino. It was monotonous, a section of the journey that marked the beginning of what was known as the "mental" part of the walk. And contrary to the classic song from *My Fair Lady*, there was no rain.

The work of the Camino journey is said to be divided into three parts. The first one is physical. The second mental and the third, spiritual. I'd become accustomed to the long days of walking, the tugging weight of my pack and even mastered the Camino shuffle. The meseta was considered the "mental" third of the journey. Long, flat and unadorned of the more scenic distractions I'd come to expect, it was every bit of what we'd been warned about. In fact, some people even opted to skip it altogether, but not me. No. I was there to walk, and I was going to walk every step. I'd passed through the first two weeks or so without much struggle. But now, for the first time, I was about to face a different kind of challenge.

Each day was much like the last. Debbie, Pat and I would leave early in the morning between 7 and 8. My pace was quicker than theirs and so after a few kilometers I would press on ahead, walking most of the morning alone. Most days, just as my stomach was beginning to long for that slice of tortilla, I would look over my shoulder and find Irish English John coming along behind me. Somehow he could sleep until 8, leave by 9 and still manage to catch up to me.

Irish English John was an even-tempered guy, with a glass half full kind of attitude. He had a long stride and I had to work hard to keep up with him. As we walked together he filled the kilometers with steady conversation. He and his wife Marg lived in a small village somewhere in the center of England. They had a married son who lived in Singapore. In the time since he'd retired, they'd spent their time with friends, traveling and tending to their beautiful garden. Irish English John was like a vanilla milkshake, pleasing, refreshing and predictably consistent. Over the miles we'd developed an ease between us, and I quickly came to rely on him.

By now I'd been on the Camino for 15 days and although I was physically tired, my heart was full. Each morning as I readied myself for the day's journey, I felt excited to begin again, ready for what was to come. It wasn't as if it hadn't been difficult. It had been. But physical challenges, no matter how taxing, had always been manageable for me. I was in labor for 36 hours with my first child, a marathon that ended in the wee hours of a cold December morning with the arrival of a 10 lbs., 1 oz. baby boy. It's true what they say about childbirth. Despite the toll that Tucker's birth took on my body, two years later I would do it all over again, this time with his brother Dylan. I remember going into labor believing I could do just about anything for 24 hours, but I had underestimated myself. I turned out, the same was true about walking.

I was still buzzing from the previous night's gathering as I got ready to leave Carrión de los Condes, my body humming with an expansiveness that was difficult to put into words. While the first two weeks were filled with the joy of new people and new adventure, I began to notice a deepening in my awareness. As I walked along, the meditation of each step gave way to a desire to dig deeper into each experience, like the opening of one of those Russian nesting dolls to find a new and more beautiful one inside. The sing-a-long with the nuns had opened my heart in a way I hadn't expected.

The next few days would take us along an old Roman road. Today I was headed to Terradillos de los Templarios, about 27 kilometers (16.5 miles) away. I filled the bladder with water and tucked it into my pack. This next stretch along the meseta would be a long one on mostly unpaved road and the word was, there weren't many places to find a refill.

It was hot as I set out, and there was little shade along the way. Before long, sweat poured down my face and stung my eyes. Although the road was flat, it was imbedded with rocks and soon my tired feet struggled to find solid footing. The scenery had taken a turn as well. The lush green vineyards of rioja gave way to brown scrub grass as far as the eye could see. It was too early in the season for the fields of sunflowers the guidebook had promised. Instead, I began to see storks nesting atop a handful of bell towers and church steeples that rose like trees into the sky.

I limped into Terradillos de los Templarios a little after 2:00 in the afternoon. Irish English John and I sat down to have our daily cervezas con limón, a pattern that was well-established by now. We ordered a couple of bocadillos de jamón to replenish our electrolytes. But before long I began to feel dizzy. Despite the heat of the late afternoon, I shivered and nausea set in.

"I'm going to go lie down," I said, turning down a third cerveza. "I'll catch up with you later."

I found my way up the steps, holding on to the banister to steady myself, and lay down in our quadruple room on the bed directly below the open window. I didn't even take off my shoes.

Debbie and Pat came in a few minutes later. "Are you OK?" they asked.

"I'm not sure," I said. "I'm feeling really dizzy all of a sudden."

"Did you have enough water to drink?"

"I think so," I said. I'd gone through my whole 1 ½ liter bladder twice after refilling it at a small café where we'd stopped to get some orange juice.

"Well just rest," Debbie said. "We're going to get something to eat and then do some laundry. I'll take yours too if you'd like."

"That would be great," I said, barely lifting my head off the bed. No sooner did I hear the click of the door behind them when I closed my eyes and fell fast asleep.

By the time we all sat down for dinner a few hours later, I was almost back to normal. In the two plus weeks I'd been on the Camino, I'd still not managed to get used to the nondescript albergue menus. It was a stretch for a self-described food snob like me. I craved the dishes Spain was known for. Savory tapas. Rich seafood paella. Even the daily slice of tortilla was a treat. But the pilgrim meals were just that. Meals. There was nothing fancy about a fried egg, a chicken cutlet or a tough piece of over-done steak let alone what passed for spaghetti. The best part of the meal as far as I was concerned was the carafe of red wine that was always included. Still, it was sustenance and it did the trick.

To my surprise, this menu included a plate of ripe melon and jamón, the fancy cured ham Spain is known for. I ordered it immediately and since it was Father's Day, we splurged on a bottle of good rioja and toasted Irish English John and Pat. The melon was like sugar, sweet and juicy. Combined with the saltiness of the ham, it was simply delicious.

The next day's walk to Mansilla de las Mulas was equally taxing. Kilometers of Roman road. Stifling heat and little shade. By mid-morning my feet began to rebel against the rocky earth. For the first time since I'd begun walking more than two weeks before, every step hurt. My feet rolled over the rocks and I found myself scouring the road ahead of me, searching for a flat place to plant them. I began to plot a path forward as if I was walking through hot coals. I maneuvered from side to side, serpentine, but nothing seemed to work. Each step became more painful than the next. Tears welled up in my eyes and I stabbed my hiking poles into the ground in frustration.

I'd brought along an audio book, Tembi Locke's beautiful memoir *From Scratch*, thinking I might listen as I walked. The story was set on the island of Sicily, the home of my paternal grandparents, but so far I hadn't listened to even a minute. There were so many people to talk to and even when I was alone, I relished the quiet. The crunch of the earth beneath my feet. The whisper of the wind. As my body moved along, I dropped into the daily meditation. But now none of that was working. I put on my headphones and allowed myself to travel to Sicily.

By the time I reached Mansilla de las Mulas, I knew I was in trouble. We'd chosen an awful albergue, the worst one of the whole Camino as far as I was concerned. The heat in the dormitory hung like a blanket that smothered my every breath and the air was thick with the acrid smell of pilgrim sweat. To make matters worse, I got stuck with a top bunk. I tossed and turned most of the night waiting for the sun to rise while I listened to my bunk mates snore.

The next morning, I awoke to learn that Debbie and Pat would be taking the bus to León. Debbie's knee continued to bother her. They'd already planned to take an extra day in the city. Since there was still a long way to go, they hoped the additional day of rest would help. The day before we'd also heard some unsettling news. A few weeks earlier, two Dutch women were walking on the approach to León when they were hit by a car driven by an inexperienced driver. One had died and the other was in critical condition.

The path of the Camino varied. While much of it meandered through small hamlets, along country roads, up mountains and across plains, the approaches to the big cities were the most difficult to maneuver. In those moments we might find ourselves walking along busy, traffic laden, multi-lane roads. Until that point I hadn't thought much about my own safety while walking, but the news of the tragedy spread like wildfire and shook some of us, making several reconsider their options. A few even made the choice to take a cab into the city, avoiding the approach altogether.

Irish English John and I grabbed a quick café con leche and left Mansilla de las Mulas together, setting out at what had become our normal quick pace, but before long I started to struggle. Although I tried my best to keep up, it soon became clear I was holding him back. My feet felt like they were being stung by a hundred bees. Each step hurt more than the last. I waved him on. "Go ahead without me," I said reluctantly. "I'll catch up with you in León."

I hobbled into town later that afternoon feeling broken and alone. The walk to the center of the city was slow and painful. I moved intentionally, one step at a time, my stride constrained as if walking through molasses, willing my feet to continue. I longed to sit down. I wanted to stop walking, but I was afraid if I did I wouldn't be able to get started again. As I passed through the city streets I trained my eyes forward and dug for every breath. Maybe it was my imagination, but the people I passed seemed to hold their gaze a bit longer than usual and their traditional "Buen Camino" had just the slightest sound of pity. I must have been quite a sight.

I needed rest. I opted to stay the night in a small hotel just outside the city wall in the center of town, a stone's throw from the cathedral. The accommodation was simple, but the thought of a solid night's sleep, a hot shower and a real towel was too good to pass up. At the same time, I was beginning to realize that I too needed a break. I booked the room for two nights.

By now my feet looked like they'd been through battle. The raw skin oozed and stuck like glue to my socks. The blisters that covered the balls and heels of both feet made it impossible to stand flat on the floor. After a shower I dug into my pack to find the needle and thread I'd brought from home and began to tend to my wounds. I poked the threaded needle through the fat part of the largest blisters cautiously, in one side and out the other. Fluid leaked from both sides. I cut the thread at both ends, leaving an inch or so of give. While the needle allowed the blisters to drain, the thread was supposed to keep it from refilling with fluid. I covered my heels and the balls of my feet with Compeed, a specialized protective bandage for blisters, and teased my sandals on.

Even with the surgery I'd done on my feet, I still could not lay them flat on the ground, let alone put my weight on them. I rolled my feet outward, bowing my legs and centering my weight on the outside edges of each foot. Although it would have made sense to stay in and rest, I was desperate to get back into town and find the others.

I walked slowly, my face grimacing in pain with each step. I wandered around by the cathedral, my eyes scanning the crowd while I looked for a familiar face. Seated in a café at the edge of the plaza, I saw Marc, the sun-bleached Aussie and Raphael, the gentle Brazilian. They'd just finished eating.

"Hey," I said as I sat down.

"How are you doing?" they asked, their eyes measuring the need for concern.

"My feet are a mess," I answered. "I'm thinking of staying an extra day to rest."

"Oh no," Raphael said. He was a petite man, dark haired and with a face that exuded kindness. He struck me as a sensitive soul, serious and thoughtful, and I was touched by his genuine concern.

"How about you? Are you guys going to stay an extra day?" I asked. Unlike many of the towns we passed through on the Camino, León was a frequent stop for tourists, with a beautiful cathedral and a number of museums to visit. I hoped they would say yes.

"I don't think so." Marc said. "I'm feeling pretty good."

"Oh," I said, trying to shield my disappointment. We chatted for a bit and then, while I worked up the courage to stand up again, they scampered off to take a trolley ride.

An hour later I met Debbie and Pat for a drink. I sent a text to Irish English John to let him know where we were. "Come join us," I said. He walked in the door a few minutes later.

The waiter came over and handed us a menu. "Donald Trump," he said with a flourish of sing-song in his voice. He rolled his "r" and added an extra emphasis on the "p". Clearly he knew an American when he saw one.

"Oh god no," Debbie, Pat and I said in unison. "We didn't vote for him." Irish English John just laughed.

"Ok then," the waiter said. "We will not mention him."

We ordered a nice bottle of rioja and a couple tapas. A charcuterie board and some pimientos de padrón, a plate of fried green peppers (*pimientos*) with a sprinkling of coarse sea salt. It was a typical Spanish tapa and a favorite of mine. Most of the peppers are mild, but every now and then you'll find one that packs a punch.

I picked up the cork from the table and held it horizontally, between my thumb and forefinger. "Do you know how to do this?" I asked. I released the cork and let it fall. It bounced once on the table and then landed on its end, standing up straight.

It was a game that took me back to warm winter evenings on Florida's Sanibel Island when the family gathered for our annual reunion at my parents' home on Parview Drive. My parents loved their wine. In fact, I could hardly remember a dinner in our house when a bottle or two wasn't on the table. My father always had two collections, one at their summer home in New Jersey and the other at their winter residence in Florida. He favored the bold Italian reds of the north, like Barbaresco and Barolo. And no bottle ever went unfinished. My mother didn't believe in putting the cork back in.

"Try it," I said, handing the cork to Pat.

We passed around the cork while I tried to convince Irish English John to stay an extra day. I was beginning to realize that if I stayed and my friends kept walking, I was going to lose them. I'd be a day behind and I wouldn't catch up. "Stay," I pleaded. "We can hang out tomorrow and see some of the town." He seemed open to the idea.

But the next morning I woke up to a text from Irish English John. "I'm walking on," he said. My heart sank.

My Camino family was falling apart. The original group that gathered that night in Estella had changed since then. After the death of Conor's friend, he and Emma returned to Dublin and Jeanette and Tim, the couple from Adelaide, left to continue their vacation along the Spanish Costa del Sol. Patrick and Maria were still with us, but like me, Patrick was struggling with blisters and it seemed likely that he'd need more than a day to rest. We'd added Irish English John, but now he was gone too.

Perhaps it hadn't mattered to the others. After all, they had each other. But the same wasn't true for me. It felt like an impossible decision. To stay behind meant letting go of the people I'd come to rely on. The faces I looked for on the walk each day. The ones I shared meals with. Sang songs with. Opened my heart to and yet the truth was, I didn't have a choice. I couldn't continue. In fact in that exact moment, I wasn't sure if I was going to finish at all.

My heart was heavy with disappointment. I'd come to depend on this group of people and to walking this journey together. Now, knowing that they were going on without me left me feeling abandoned and sorry for myself. Irish English John's departure was the final straw. I couldn't help but think that if someone had asked me to wait, I would have done so in an instant. I didn't understand why the same wasn't true for me.

But walking together had never been promised. Those were my expectations, ones that had appeared without me even realizing it. Looking back, I am struck by how often it happened. Expectations that crept in without me even realizing it. These were my beliefs. About family. Friendship. Loyalty and commitment. Expectations I didn't even know I had. They colored my experience and made it difficult to be fully present. My friends' decision to walk on had nothing to do with me. They had every right to walk their own Camino as I did to walk mine.

Later that day, while my friends continued on to the next town, I limped into the local pilgrim shop to see what I could do to take care of my feet. The shopkeeper smiled, greeting us as we walked in. "Hola. Necessitas ayudar?" *Do you need help?*

"Si, por favor," I said, pointing to my feet. "Yo tengo ampollas. *I have blisters.* Muchisimas ampollas."

The shopkeeper laughed. He walked out from behind the counter and up to a large display of socks that took up the entire wall of the small shop. "Necessitas un par de estos calcetines," he said. *You need these socks.*

"Que?" I asked. Perhaps he hadn't understood my question. "Yo tengo muchas ampollas," I repeated.

He smiled at me and handed me a pair of black socks from the display.

"Hablas ingles?" I was confused. This was definitely not working. My feet were raw with blisters. I could barely stand. A pair of socks was certainly not going to help me.

"Yes," he said. "I speak English. You want these socks. They will help you, I promise."

"Socks?"

He nodded. "Take off all your bandages. The Compeed. Everything. Put sock to skin. You'll thank me. I promise."

I looked at him suspiciously. I wondered how many unsuspecting peregrinos he'd pitched with the same spiel. "OK," I said, my voice betraying my distrust. "How much are they?" The truth was, at that point I was in so much pain I was willing to try anything.

"30 euro," he said.

I bought two pair.

The following morning I awoke to a text from Bob. I'd called him the night before, sending along a photo of my ailing feet. "Good morning," it said. "We hope your feet feel better. We wish we could loan you ours." Attached was a picture of two sets of paws.

I smiled. "Thanks" I texted back. "I'll be OK. I miss you guys." I pulled on my magic socks, slipped my backpack on my back and set out again.

Journal Entry

Day 21 - León to San Martín del Camino

25.4 kilometers (15.2 miles) New socks on, I hobbled my way to San Martín with a Cuban guy named Benny who lives in Tampa. The road was awful. Along the freeway for most of it. Still storks in the bell towers. Small earth covered bodegas. And more yellow arrows.

Made it to the albergue in time to watch a big rainstorm come in. Hung out for a while under the covers

141

while Debbie and Pat did laundry. I'm feeling really wiped out. A big family dinner at the albergue with a bunch of brand new people. New countries, new languages. Names I will never remember.

Day 22 - San Martín del Camino to Astorga

23.1 kilometers (13.9 miles) Finally off the road and into some beautiful scenery. We walked across a beautiful stone bridge, and came across a snack stand where we ran into Maria and Jarah. We took a rest there and had a glass of lemonade. I loved the sign on the stand. "La llave de la esencia es la presencia." The key to essence is presence.

Once we got to Astorga we toured another Gothic cathedral and the Palacio Gaudí which has a museum. My camera broke, which is really a disappointment. Guess I'll be taking pictures with my phone from here on in.

Day 23 - Astorga to Foncebadón

25.9 kilometers (16.1 miles) Today would have been my Dad's 84th birthday. Said goodbye to Debbie and Pat this morning as they will take a bus to Ponferrada —Even though I left very early, Debbie got up to give me a hug goodbye.

A long slow climb back into the mountains. Through wonderful small towns filled with stone houses, laughter and leisurely walking breaks. More amazing wildflowers and spectacular views.

Had a wonderful Camino dinner with Benny, Melissa and Kwang at the albergue in Foncebadón. I was so happy to see Kwang again!

DAY 24
FONCEBADÓN
KILOMETER 544

CHAPTER 11

Prayers

The early morning rain fell gently as Benny and I left the albergue in Foncebadón, walking under a canopy of dark clouds. Today we would pass the highest point on the whole journey before making the descent into the village of Ponferrada.

We'd met two days before as I hobbled out of San Martin del Camino. Even with the day of rest in León and the pair of magic socks, the blisters on the bottom of my feet were raw, and pain shot through my legs with each and every step. Benny was a Cuban immigrant who lived in Florida. He was stocky, solidly built with a thick head of grey hair and neatly trimmed facial hair. Benny was meticulously dressed, in sky blue gym shorts and a matching baseball style cap. He'd begun the Camino with his daughter who'd since met a group of like-minded folks and was now a few days behind him.

It was our third day of walking together. Like me, Benny had his own share of blisters and a bad knee too. In the beginning, we'd made great walking partners. Misery loves company, they say. We walked slowly, chatting away to keep our minds off the excruciating pain that came with every step. Benny had a large family, a wife and three daughters of whom he was very proud. He was a cabinet maker, a lover of lighthouses and an avid movie buff. He was warm and attentive and, like me, someone who felt things deeply. Benny had a habit of letting out a sigh now and then, accompanied by an "Oh my god," when the pain got to be too intense.

I understood this, of course. When I was growing up, my mother christened me "Eeyore," mistaking my high sensitivity for the dysthymic depression personified by Milne's famous donkey. Of course, I did not agree with her assessment. I was simply speaking my truth but certain truths were not something that was welcome in my family, especially if they didn't line up with those of my mother. Looking back, I'm convinced my grumbling was a reaction to a feeling of not being seen. Over the years I became overly conscious of my tendency to complain when the going got tough. It was a practice I'd worked hard to grow out of, and as a result, I found myself highly reactive when I happened to be in the company of another Eeyore.

Now, four days after I'd put on the magic socks, the pain began to diminish. I picked up my pace, attacking the trail in a manner more similar to the early days of walking. At the top of the hill I stopped to wait for Benny and turned my eyes to the deep, blue grey and forest green vistas that spread out before us. There was a band of light in the distance, an indication of drier miles ahead, but for now, we were stuck with what we had.

Ahead of us stood the *Cruz de Ferro*, the Iron Cross. If there was a moment I'd anticipated along the Camino, this was it. The *Cruz* was a crude site, especially against the dark and dreary sky: an iron cross atop a tall wooden pole surrounded by a huge mound of rocks. But in the early morning quiet it felt as holy as any church I'd been in along the way.

No one knew for certain the origin of the site. Over the years the tradition of leaving a stone to symbolize the releasing of one's burdens had developed, but as I looked at it now, there were all sorts of things left behind. Flags, stuffed animals, bouquets of plastic flowers. As I'd prepared to walk the Camino, I'd collected a stone from my yard and painted my mother and father's names on it, Beatrice Marie Basili and Thomas Edward Maggio. It would be my offering when I reached the iron cross. I tucked it in the outside pocket of my pack and there it remained for the first 22 days of my journey.

We stood in the quiet and waited for a group of pilgrims to finish their visit to this makeshift altar. Benny motioned for me to go first. I unzipped the small pocket on my hip strap and removed the stone I'd carried from home. The rockpile clattered beneath my feet as I found my way up to the top and stood for a few moments to look at the contributions left by others. Who knew how long any of them had been there, layered atop each other for years, a vast collection of memories, hopes and dreams of nameless, faceless pilgrims who had come long before me. I knelt down and bowed my head, feeling a holiness in the moment. A sea of nonspecific images and emotion overwhelmed me, sensations jumbled together like the rocks beneath my feet. "I love you Mom and Dad," I whispered as I released my stone to the ground.

Tears mixed with rain as I made my way back to Benny. "Are you OK?" he asked. I nodded, unable to speak. With a jumble of emotion still caught in my throat, I turned and watched Benny make his way to the cross.

My body tingled, my cells vibrating with memories of my parents. It's hard to explain but as I stood there, in this unfamiliar place, I felt surrounded by them in that moment. And although I stood alone, the rain hitting my face and my feet touching the earth below me, I was aware of an expansiveness, a deep connection to what had come before.

We stood there for a while, reluctant to leave. Soon, the sky began to brighten. Another group of pilgrims were waiting to approach the cross so we continued on, walking away in silence. Soon, Benny fell behind and I was alone again, lost in my memories. I missed Debbie and Pat, Irish English John and the rest of my Camino family; Marc, Raphael and the others. By now they were all a full day ahead of me. Irish English John had been sending me scouting reports from the road, making recommendations about albergues and places to get a bite to eat. There were eight more days until I reached Santiago.

I was growing frustrated with Benny's complaining. I'd willingly appointed myself his cheerleader, my energies focused on getting him through each day. Words of encouragement poured from my lips at every opportunity. "You're doing great. Keep going. You've got this." I'd taken on the responsibility of securing lodging for both of us each night. I was doing it for myself anyway, it was just as easy to reserve two beds instead of one. In the beginning it had been easy. I was happy to keep his spirits up. But, as the days wore on and Benny's struggles continued, I became frustrated. I found myself suffering from compassion fatigue. After all, all my cheering him on didn't seem to be helping.

The magic of the socks was working. I was able to move more quickly, my feet finally free of the pain that had plagued me since León. The stronger I got, the more I began to feel burdened by the responsibility I felt to take care of him. I didn't want to do it anymore, but I didn't dare admit it out loud. I felt guilty and selfish for wanting to focus less on him and more on my own journey. It wasn't his fault. He was struggling. I was the one who'd decided to be his cheerleader, who'd taken on that responsibility. He hadn't asked me to do it. I'd done what I'd believed to be the right thing to do. To support a friend when he needed it most. Ironically, it was the thing I'd hoped others would have done for me.

I wondered if it was possible to care for others and still take care of myself. How often I'd been faced with that struggle in my life. It was an old behavior, one that I'd learned at a very young age. As a child I'd learned to sacrifice my needs for the needs of others. Did it have to be that way? Wasn't there a way to do both?

And why not tell Benny how I felt? Certainly he would have understood. But I didn't have the courage. I didn't want to hurt him, of that I was sure. My frustrations were my own. He was doing the best he could. And so I kept quiet. Now I wonder what might have happened if I'd made a different choice.

I decided to find a single room the next night. I'd be more patient after a good night of sleep, I told myself. I'd take a break and then we'd continue on together again.

I took a room at the Posada Plaza Mayor, a small hotel on the square in Villafranca del Bierzo. It was, to date, the nicest place I'd stayed on the Camino, one worthy of the tinge of guilt I felt for treating myself to what now felt like opulence. Three weeks into the Camino what passed for luxury were really the basic comforts in life, things I'd always taken for granted. A bed made with cotton sheets. Real towels that covered your whole body. A bathroom where you could close the door and be alone. This place took the cake. It even had a bathtub.

I drew a bath and eased my tired body into the tub. I must have fallen asleep because the next thing I knew, the water was cold and my fingers were shriveled like raisins. I climbed out of the tub, got dressed and went off to explore.

"Hola," I said to the man sitting just outside the hotel. Since I began the journey in St-Jean, I'd continued to make a point to speak to as many people as possible. I'd come a long way from my first timid effort with Debbie and Pat. The struggle I'd felt in the beginning eased as the miles wore on and after 20 plus days, my reticence had all but disappeared. It was easier than I'd expected. Everyone was so welcoming and kind, and most of them met me with a smile. By now saying hello was almost second nature.

"Buen Camino," he said.

"You're American. I'd recognize that accent anywhere." I laughed.

"Right on the money." He smiled. "I'm from California, from the San Francisco Bay Area. My name is Robert."

"No kidding," I said. He was virtually a neighbor of mine.

He was walking with a church group who'd been studying the Ignatian Spiritual Exercises, a series of Christian prayers, meditations and reflections to help someone discover the will of God in their lives. He wondered if I'd heard of them.

"Of course," I said, a familiar bell ringing in my memory. "I'm Jesuit educated." Although I'd never studied the Spritual Exercises myself, I'd been introduced to Jesuit teachings first while I was a student at Boston College and then after I graduated and began a year of national service with the Jesuit Volunteer Corps.

I wore my Jesuit education like a badge of honor. It was the catalyst for my career as a social worker, for a life dedicated in service to others. It was my experience at Boston College that led me to Montana, first as a Jesuit Volunteer working in Great Falls and then to the Northern Cheyenne Reservation where I worked as a counselor for Native kids in a group home. I'd taken to heart the focus on service that was part of the Jesuit values. I chose a career focused on social justice, determined to make a difference in the world.

But as I stood there in the late afternoon sun, I felt a tug on my heartstrings, a longing for something I had not yet realized. As much as I connected with Jesuit teaching around social justice, I felt divorced from my Catholic faith. In my final two years in college, I'd been part of a strong community of people to whom practicing their faith had been a regular part of living. But even as I joined in, I felt a distance from it, like I was missing something. There were times I felt glimmers of something, like the way the sunlight peeks through the opening in an old oak tree. But then the wind blows. The branches move. The sun sits higher in the sky. The moment is gone. As much as I enjoyed the time spent together and the bonds we formed, I knew I didn't have the same commitment to my faith as the others did. Perhaps, not surprisingly, as I got older and moved away from the culture and people of my early years, so did my practice. I no longer went to church regularly, and other than saying grace at dinner, I rarely prayed. Those traditions lost their significance long ago.

"I've struggled with my faith for a long time," I confessed to him. "I guess a part of me is hoping that I'll get some clarity as I walk, but so far, it hasn't come."

"Are you open to what you might find?" I broke his gaze, turning my eyes downward. I felt exposed, as if I'd just showed him more than I'd intended. "You can't just wait to discover, you have to ask the questions. That's the way you find the answers." Robert looked at his watch. "I've got to go. I'm meeting the others for our afternoon discussion. It was really nice meeting you. I'll pray for you, that you find your purpose in walking."

I set out the next morning for Herrerías early. Before I'd gone to bed, I'd received a text from Benny to let me know that he was going to stay in Villafranca and wait for his daughter to catch up. He could use an extra day or two of rest, he'd said, if he was going to make it the rest of the way. I couldn't help but wonder if he'd sensed my frustration. Although my guilt still lingered, I was grateful for the chance to continue on knowing that he wouldn't be alone. I knew how much he'd wanted to walk with his daughter, and how disappointed he'd been when she'd chosen to lag behind. I was glad he'd be able to finish the journey with her.

"Buen Camino," I texted back. "Have a good walk. See you in Santiago."

For the past few days the path had taken us down narrow streets through beautiful stone villages. Old wooden doors painted in bright colors welcomed visitors. Sprays of vibrant geraniums poured out of pots that lined the streets and blossoms dripped from balconies above. For the first time in a while, my feet no longer ached with every step. I breathed in the beauty of it all. I felt peaceful today. The birds chirping, the water rushing in the stream, I could hardly stop myself from smiling.

In Trabadelo I stopped for a midmorning café con leche. "Can I join you?" I asked a young, dark haired American who was sitting alone.

"Of course," she said. "I'm Sam."

"Suzanne. Nice to meet you. How's it going?" I set my cup on the table and sat down across from her. I had to admit I was proud of myself. Before the Camino I would have looked for an empty table. Although I considered myself an extrovert, I was shy when it came to new situations. Choosing to walk alone had forced me to step out of my comfort zone. Now, situations that had once felt difficult were much easier.

"Great," she said, her blue eyes sparkling with excitement. "It's so beautiful here, isn't it?"

I nodded. "Are you walking alone?"

"No. My friend Erin and I are making the pilgrimage together." She motioned to a woman sitting with a group of others at a nearby table. "We've challenged ourselves to reach out to people, to spread light as we walk." Sam bubbled with enthusiasm. Her face hopeful. Joy radiated from her, the way sunlight dances on a mountain lake. "We've been praying the rosary this morning."

I smiled as I remembered a trip I'd taken when I was a Jesuit Volunteer. I'd found myself in a car with a group of elderly nuns on our way to Hays, Montana. The sisters were going to a retreat, and I asked if I could tag along to visit a friend.

It was a four-hour drive from Great Falls to Hays. Even with my early training, that was a long time for my 21-year-old self to make small talk with anyone; let alone with a bunch of 70 something nuns - who I liked, by the way. A lot. An hour or so into our journey, Sister Marina pulled out her rosary beads. For those who didn't grow up Catholic, the rosary is a set of devotional prayers organized in decades (10 prayers) around a series of mysteries in the life of Christ. It is recited with a string of beads that serve as a way of keeping track of the prayers. After reciting the opening prayers, Sister Marina handed the set of rosary beads to Sister Grace who sat next to her. Evidently, this was going to be a group activity. I started to panic.

There's nothing worse than being exposed for the fraud that you are. As a lifelong Catholic (and now a Jesuit volunteer) I was embarrassed to admit I didn't know how to pray the rosary, let alone know anyone besides my grandmother who did it regularly. I knew, of course, the *Hail Mary* and the *Our Father*, prayers I'd recited since I was a child, but the rosary has all sorts of other parts to it. Mysteries and additional prayers and rules about what you say and when. I was sunk.

Of course, I needn't have worried. The sisters couldn't have been kinder. Sr. Grace handed the beads to me. They were praying the Joyful mysteries. "The fourth mystery," she said, reading the dread in my face. "Is the presentation of Jesus in the temple."

I slid my hand over the next bead and swallowed hard "Our Father, who art in heaven, hallowed be they name." The sisters joined in. I breathed a sigh of relief.

Sam laughed. "I still don't know how to say it," I confessed.

There was something familiar about her, a simplicity that took me back to that time. As we sat across the small metal table, sharing coffee and stories, I saw myself in her, a part of me I recognized from long ago. A piece I'd lost somewhere along the way.

I'd made the decision to join the Jesuit Volunteer Corps right after college, much to the disappointment of my parents who'd hoped I go straight to graduate school. More than a decision, it was a calling, a knowing that reverberated from every part of my body. It was a transformative year, one that I spent living and working with a group of women from all across the country. There were seven of us in all, assigned to a variety of nonprofits around town. We shared a house. A checkbook. Chores and meals. But more than that, we committed to being a community. A faith-based community that prayed together. Attended mass regularly. Went on retreats and read scripture. I even worked with the church youth group.

And I liked it. All of it. Baking bread for Sunday communion. Coaching the youth group as they prepared for Palm

Sunday Mass. Getting to know the parish priests. In that year I'd formed a connection to my faith I'd never known before. It wasn't my parents' or my grandparents' faith or the faith of the *Baltimore Catechism* I'd learned as a child or even the faith I'd been taught in high school. *That* faith was rote. Hollow and without meaning, filled with shoulds and have-tos and obligations. *This* faith was personal. For the first time in my life I felt a deep visceral connection to God and it filled me with joy.

But it was short-lived. As the years passed, I could not sustain the connection, disappointed by a church that failed time and time again to live up to the Gospel it preached. I found the services lifeless. The actions of the institution hypocritical. I longed for inspiration, for a way to tie the life I was living to the words of the pastors, but too often they left me feeling detached and remote. So too was our church community. On Sunday people streamed in and out, occasionally stopping for a smile and a quick hello. But like everything else, it too, felt hollow.

And still I went through the motions. I baptized my children and dragged them, sometimes kicking and screaming, to Mass. I taught catechism for a while, doing my best to bring to life a spirituality I believed in, of kindness, hope and service to others. But even as I did my best to stay connected, I was watching it slip away. It had been hard enough to reckon with the blatant homophobia of the church, a church that would not allow my brother and so many others to marry the people they loved, and then came the child sexual abuse scandal and the defensiveness, lying and cover-up that followed. It disgusted me and filled me with shame. How could I stay part of a church that would treat its own people that way? I felt adrift, not knowing where to turn. I hadn't lost my faith in God, but rather in the institution itself.

Eventually I gave up. I stopped going to church. Stopped forcing my kids to participate in something that had no meaning for them. I still identified as Catholic, but without the rituals that once rooted me to my faith, I wondered if it could still be true. The term 'cafeteria Catholic' came to mind, a term often used to describe people who picked and chose what they wanted to follow. But I'd already been doing that, hadn't I? What was it that still tied me to my Catholic faith?

And then a few years ago, I was having a conversation with my youngest son. He didn't believe in God, he said. It broke my heart although I suppose it shouldn't have come as a surprise. I felt like I'd failed him. It was hard to expect him to believe in something I was struggling to believe in myself. Although I wanted him to have a faith, to believe in something bigger than himself, I understood. The Church had little to offer someone Dylan's age. I'd hoped he'd find his own connection to God, perhaps apart from organized religion. Maybe he still would. In truth, wasn't that what I was still working on myself?

"How long have you been walking," I asked Sam. I was surprised I hadn't seen her before.

"Just a few days," she said, "We started just two days ago in Astorga, but we plan to continue on to Santiago."

I began to tell her about the experience I'd had in Carrión de los Condes, about the singing nuns and the deep sense of connection I felt as we shared our journeys with one another. About the way the room reverberated with hope when we sang. About the tears that came from a place deep inside me, a feeling I did not yet understand.

"I want to give you something," I said to Sam. I reached into my pack and pulled out the star that the sisters had given me. "The sisters gave us this after the pilgrim Mass. It was to remind us that we are the light. That we are called to bring light to others. One by one, with everyone we meet, just like what you and Erin are doing." I felt a lump in my throat as I repeated the words that resonated so deeply with me. "And to remember," I continued, "That when we join together, we can light up even the darkest night." Tears filled my eyes as I handed it to her.

Sam smiled and pressed her hand to her heart as she took the small paper star. "Thank you," she said. "That's so beautiful. I'll treasure this."

I finished my coffee and bid Sam goodbye. "Buen Camino," I said. "Hope to see you again down the road."

"Me too," she smiled. "Thanks again for sharing your star with me."

As I walked away, I felt a spark rekindle deep inside. It was as if I were hearing a native language, one I hadn't spoken in quite some time. The words were still there, a bit rusty perhaps, but I hadn't forgotten. I smiled to myself as I thought back to the conversation I'd had on the steps of the hotel in Villafranca del Bierzo just the day before. A chance meeting with a stranger who'd promised to pray for me.

He had sent Sam to me.

Journal Entry

Day 26 - Villafranca – Las Herrerías

20.5 kilometers (12.4 miles) An unintentionally short day after arriving in Herrerías at noon unable to cancel the reservation. It was OK though. I did laundry and took a shower. The hotel is very pretty and the little village is very sweet, cows roaming in the field across from me, a stream rushes nearby and there is an occasional crack of thunder.

I passed through so many lovely villages today. Stone buildings dripping with flowers. As I came into Her-rerías, I passed over a bridge and found a tree covered in ribbons... It was a dream tree, and there was a sign encouraging passers-by to hang their dreams on its branches. "With an open heart and a quiet mind, there are no doors."

I am sitting at a café as I write, and I just saw the most remarkable sight. A family just walked by, a mom and dad, 4 children, and two donkeys! They are pilgrims... they have shells hanging from their backpacks... The donkeys are saddled with big leather bags, perhaps carrying the children's belongings... such an extraordinary sight!

It's interesting how little we really need on the Camino. It's of course nice to have a little more, but at the same time, the simplicity of life on the Camino, the sustenance required to continue each day — to eat, sleep, walk, (have purpose) and community. Community that can be forged anywhere — in any language in any amount of time. In the course of one day — or one hour. I had a wonderful conversation with a mom of 4 girls from Ohio — and then a couple of doctors from Cologne, Germany who invited me to share their dinner table with them. I had a delicious dinner of bacalao and two desserts — at the insistence of the owner who suggested I needed it for O Cebreiro.

Day 27 - Herrerías to Triacastela

28.9 kilometers (18 miles)This was a long, long day. We climbed O Cebreiro, the highest point on the Camino in Spain. The scenery was breathtaking. We crossed into Galicia. At the top of the mountain I stopped to eat lunch and had my first taste of queso con miel, a delicious cheese served with honey and bread. I said hello to a couple of young women and ended up sharing my cheese with them.

After the long walk over the Pyrenees, O Cebreiro did not really seem that difficult. Perhaps I'm just in much better shape.

Ran into a gang of cows in the street and many loose and very big dogs that looked more like miniature horses. The descent into Triacastela was difficult. Steep and long. I got to the albergue and immediately lay down for an hour to recuperate before taking my shower and doing laundry. I stayed in a beautifully renovated stone building, but, as is usual for the shared living spaces, I didn't get a restful night of sleep due to the lack of privacy and needing to sleep in my clothes which I just can't get comfortable with. Not to mention the heat in the room with all those bodies.

I wandered into town to find a pharmacy and a bank and ran into Annabella and her friends and joined them for a glass of wine. We met in Villafranca when we were both looking for a way to get into the convent Santa Maria. Annabella is a Venezuelan who lives in New York City. Warm and affectionate, she invited me to sit and eat with them. We shared a plate of pimientos de padrón, although they weren't very hot.

I am amazed that we are so close to finishing. I am amazed that my body has been able to walk so many miles. I feel so many things. Excited – proud – awe – exhausted – sad - grateful. I am very, very, grateful. I am very, very, sad.

Day 28 - Triacastela – Barbadelo

29.5 kilometers (18.33 miles) Through Sarria and on to the final stretch. Took the long way to Sarria via the beautiful Benedictine monastery in Samos which had a great tour (in Spanish). It was a mixture of baroque and other styles but suffered terrible damage due to two fires. Only the cloister, chapel and façade remain. Spent the walk with a young woman from Barcelona and spoke Spanish the whole time – feeling very proud of my ability to carry on a conversation, despite all the mistakes I make and my very limited vocabulary.

Passed through Sarria, up the "Escalante duro" which I lovingly renamed the "are you fucking kidding me" staircase until landing in the tiny little town of Barbadelo. All along the way now there are elaborate grain stores. They are long and narrow, often set high in the air on pillars. They are ornate, with turrets and spires and made of beautiful stone. At first I didn't know what they were, thinking that maybe they we some sort of shrine, but I learned that they are used to hold grain and ripen all different kinds of produce.

Passed the 100 kilometer marker and stopped to take a picture. That's all we have left to go.

Day 29 - Barbadelo – Castromaior

27 kilometers (16.8 miles) I met Cameron for coffee (the girls didn't show up) and we head out. The weather was cool and comfortable for most of the morning. Cameron's pace was much quicker than mine so after a while, I said goodbye and continued on alone. Through small villages and beautiful lush Galician countryside. Gardens overflowing with kale and potatoes, surrounded with stone gates and fences –

The day started off cool but by midday the heatwave that is gripping the EU caught us too. By Portomarin, I was hoping to get some food but the trail bypassed the town. I caught up with Adrianna (from Sao Paolo) and we walked together. The sun was quite hot and I was out of water so the final kilometers were very difficult. We were both hungry and thirsty and very hot... until we came across a small café – with lots of flies – but the beer was cold!

The hostal is Castromaior was simple, a group of women from New Mexico checked in as well as two women from the Canary Islands. I had dinner with the women at the one and only café in town. I had salad as I'd eaten earlier, but enjoyed the women's company as well as my first slice of torta de Santiago, the local almond cake.

DAY 30
MELIDE
KILOMETER 725.7

CHAPTER 12

Ave Maria

Despite the fact that every muscle in my body felt like a bowl of lime green jello, I'd promised to meet Adriana and Ian for dinner. Adriana was an astrologist of sorts, a tarot card, palm reading, horoscope loving woman from Buenos Aires who was outgoing, playful and decidedly offbeat. Adriana was also opinionated and bold. She'd been walking with Ian, a staid, elder Brit who seemed marginally depressed and who I first met at the albergue in San Martin del Camino. Ian was the polar opposite of Adriana, serious, somber and thoughtful. Perhaps that's what made them good walking partners.

As we walked the 31 kilometers (18.6 miles) to Melide, we bantered back and forth about how we handled people whose views were different than ours. "I think it's important to tolerate them." Adriana had said.

"Tolerate? I think it's important to offer acceptance," said Ian, who was every bit of an English gentleman.

"I'm with Ian," I said. "I think acceptance is preferable to tolerance. When you tolerate someone, it means you're just kind of putting up with them. To tolerate implies judgement. It feels dismissive, like you're not open to their views at all."

"Agreed," said Ian.

"No," Adriana weighed in. "You're both wrong. Tolerance is better than acceptance. When you tolerate someone, you don't have to accept their view. You're just saying it's whatever they think. They can have their thoughts. You don't have to agree."

"You don't have to agree to accept," Ian said, the frustration in his voice mounting. "That's the whole point of acceptance."

And so it continued for 10 long kilometers.

The bottoms of my feet pulsed as I lay motionless on the bottom bunk of the large room I shared with two young Italians who had been walking the Camino Primitivo. Unlike the Camino Frances, the Primitivo route is the oldest of the Camino routes, the one that King Alfonso is said to have followed to Santiago. It began in the region of Asturias, in the town of Oviedo, and travelled west to Lugo and then south to Santiago, joining the Camino Frances here, in the town of Melide.

We were getting closer to the end. Ever since Sarria, The Way had been filled with new faces, with pilgrims who were walking the final 100 kilometers to Santiago as well as those who had walked other routes. The Camino del Norte. The Camino Portuguese. And now here, the Camino Primitivo. The Italians seemed nice enough, a couple from the north. He spoke some English. She did not. We chatted for a few minutes while we struggled to open the window in the room together. They left to take showers and I lay down on the bed, exhausted. I dozed off and then woke in a panic. I checked my watch. It was 6:00 p.m.

I willed myself off the bottom bunk, slid on my sandals and made my way back into town. I found Adriana and Ian sitting outside a café with a group of Americans, a family of five from Oklahoma. I met Jessica, the mother and her three children, a day earlier outside Portomarin. Matt, the dad, had since joined them. They would walk the final kilometers together. I ordered the biggest cerveza con limón I could carry and pulled up a seat beside them.

They'd made a reservation at a restaurant just a few feet away. I hoped I could get pulpo (octopus) which is a specialty in the region of Galicia. We gathered around a long table on the patio, just outside the kitchen. The 3 kids at one end and the adults at the other. I took a seat next to one of their two daughters. When the waitress came around, I ordered Pulpo á la Gallega, boiled octopus on toast, drizzled with olive oil and tomato. We ordered two bottles of the local vino tinto for the table.

I wondered what it was like to walk the Camino with your children. More than once I'd wished my boys were with me, a feeling I frequently had when I travelled. I longed to share what I was seeing and experiencing with them. At the end of each day I sent them pictures, hoping to give them just a glimpse of this incredible journey, but Jessica got to experience it with hers. How lucky she was.

At the same time, I wondered what it was like for *them*? They were of high school age, the point at which they might want to be anywhere but with their mother and father on a 500-mile hike in Spain. They might be surly. Staring at their cell phones. Embarrassed by their parents. Responding to questions from overly curious strange adults with nothing more than a grunt.

But not these kids. These kids were delightful. They were articulate and funny. They answered my questions thoughtfully. Expansively. They had their own opinions, of course. They teased each other playfully and there was the occasional wisecrack, but they really were lovely. And what's more, they seemed to really like each other.

I've worked with enough teenagers to know how unusual this was. In some ways they reminded me of my siblings and me. Since my father's career as an elected official began when I was just eight years old and my youngest brother only four, we were regularly in the company of adults. We'd spent our weekends at political events and public gatherings and often we were the only kids in the room. We'd campaigned for him, canvassed neighborhoods and made telephone calls to solicit voter support from campaign headquarters. When we left the house, my parents were quick to remind us that we were on public display.

As my father's business career grew, he took us to international conferences in Spain, Sicily and Yugoslavia. Once again, we were the only children in the room. We had no choice but to learn quickly how to comport ourselves in the company of adults. How to carry on a conversation. Be respectful and make eye contact. Upon returning home my mother would grade our behavior, giving us a report card of sorts. She referenced the comments of her friends as evidence and the bar was always set high.

Perhaps not surprisingly, I hadn't appreciated it back then. It was normal, life as we knew it, although, to be honest, sometimes it felt like a burden. But as far as we were concerned, we had no choice. It was our responsibility to make our parents proud. A show of love and respect for them. But as I've gotten older and had children of my own, I understood now just how unusual it was.

The kids told me that their mom was a trained opera singer. As they'd walked the Camino, they would stop in churches along the way and Jessica would sing the *Ave Maria*.

"Wow!" I said. I was struck by the courage it took to do something like that. "How was that?"

"Amazing," one of the daughters said, her face beaming as she looked at her mother. "The acoustics in the old churches are incredible. People stop and listen. She has an amazing voice."

"Would you sing for us?" I asked.

Jessica smiled, her head tilting slightly. She looked over at Matt who gave a wink and an encouraging smile. And then she began to sing.

Ave Maria / Gratia plena / Maria gratia plena/ Maria gratia plena...

A few notes in and I am gone.

Images flash through my mind like snapshots in a photo album. Yellowed. Smokey. The color slightly off. It is 1986 and I am twenty-six years old and about to get married.

I have returned home to plan my wedding. There is never any discussion about where I will be married. I was born and raised on the East Coast. My family still lives there. My parents and sister in New Jersey. One brother in Pennsylvania, the other in Massachusetts. Aunts, uncles, and grandparents fill in the spaces from Maryland to New York. Despite the fact that I have lived in California for more than 3 years now, it never occurs to me to be married anywhere else.

My mother and I are standing at the entrance to her country club, the place she has chosen for the reception. We have already been to the florist. I want color, not the traditional white bouquet, but despite my resistance, my mother convinces me to include white

Stephanotis, a flower she had in her wedding bouquet. They will be added to the pink-centered Rubrum lilies and deep purple Irises that I have chosen. Anne, my dearest childhood friend, has an uncle who is a priest. He has agreed to marry us in his parish.

The country club seems fine, a beautiful setting with lush green rolling lawns that seem to stretch for miles. The manager greets us at the door and shows us into a big room filled with tables. "This is where the bar will go," he says, pointing to a corner of the room opposite the large wall of windows that overlook the seventh hole. We will eat Beef Wellington and dance in the center of the room on a large parquet dance floor.

I am finalizing decisions that my mother has already made. I have let my mother take the lead on much of this. She has found the place, the florist and the band. I am grateful for her help. It is challenging, I tell myself, to plan a wedding from across the country. But as the preparations continue, I begin to realize the wedding is more a reflection of her than it is of me.

A week earlier my mother and I talked through the ceremony on the telephone.

"The organist will play the Ave Maria as you walk down the aisle," my mother says.

"I don't want the Ave Maria, Mom." I want something contemporary. I'd hoped to be married outdoors with guitar music but the Catholic Church will not allow an outdoor wedding. Elisa, my sister and Lynn, my dear friend from my year as Jesuit Volunteer, will play the guitar and sing.

"I love the Ave Maria," my mother says. "It's the song I entered to when your father and I got married."

"I don't want that kind of wedding, Mom. I don't need an organist. Elisa and Lynn are going to sing." I had chosen some of my favorite contemporary songs, music that reminded me of my year as a Jesuit Volunteer.

165

"Elisa and Lynn are going to be walking in right before you. You're going to need an organist to play when you walk into the church. It's a beautiful song."

She was right. Still. "I don't want the Ave Maria," I said.

My mother gets quiet, the kind of silence that always filled me with guilt. A silence that lets me know she is wounded. I have been wounding my mother for more years than I can count.

It was a familiar dance. A mother and her oldest daughter. A battle of personalities. Hers larger than life. Dynamic and forceful. The lead in every play. Mine, oddly pubescent. Squeaky. Unsure. Despite my age I am still afraid to step into the breech with her. I am accustomed to being the supporting cast and I have learned the role well.

My mother did not share the stage easily. Even, as it turned out, when it was my own wedding. Because that's where I was wrong. I was, of course, the one that was getting married, but it was her party. My parents were paying for this extravaganza, she reminded me more than once. I would be allowed to make decisions about what I wanted so long as it did not conflict with what she wanted.

I hung up the phone. I felt frustrated and angry but also guilty. I'd never learned to hold on to my power when she was concerned. I always acquiesced, choosing familial harmony over my own desires. I didn't want the Ave Maria, dammit. What was so hard to understand about that?

But as the wedding got closer, I called the organist. "Would you play the Ave Maria," I asked, "After communion. It is one of my mother's favorite songs." I would surprise her. I would be a good daughter.

After the wedding, I asked if she'd heard it. She hadn't said anything and I was waiting for an acknowledgement of my gift to her.

"Yes," she said. Her answer was understated. Matter of fact. Perhaps she'd expected me to give in, but I hadn't thought of it

that way. I'd done it to make her happy. To let her know I appreciated everything she was doing for me. Once again, I waited for an acknowledgement that would never come.

Now, as I sat at this café in Melide, tears filled my eyes as I listened to Jessica sing. My mother had been dead for three years. Although I'd since let go of the anger that had marked my relationship with her, I couldn't help but think about how ridiculous that argument was, how so many of our battles had been. It was not an improper request. It was my wedding, I had the right to plan it as I saw fit. But my mother was egocentric and our world revolved around her. She demanded that of us, and so I did what I could to keep the peace. To do what I thought she wanted. To make her proud. I'd spent so much of my life waiting to be acknowledged for who I was, a separate individual from her with my own wishes, hopes and dreams. So much of it filled with the pain of longing for something that would never come. I was grateful to have finally moved on.

As Jessica sang, a crowd began to gather around the table. The owners of the restaurant and the kitchen staff, dressed in the food-stained whites that bore the evidence of a busy night's work, came out to listen. As she hit the final notes of the *Ave Maria*, the restaurant exploded in applause.

"Bravo!" the crowd yelled. "Bravo." Jessica smiled.

"Please sing another," we asked.

She began to sing again, this time an aria from Puccini's La Bohéme, "*Quando me'n Vo'*".

On Sunday afternoons, after we attended Mass and had our breakfast, my parents would retire to the living room to read the Sunday paper. They always took two papers, the local *Courier News* and the *New York Times*. The Sunday crossword puzzle in the New York Times was legendary, the most difficult one of the week. Centered around abstract themes and filled with complex clues, it was, not surprisingly, my mother's favorite. She'd plant herself on the green leather couch in the living room, pen in hand and an empty ash tray by her side and she would get to work. Hours later, having uncovered the hidden theme and the ashtray now overflowing with spent cigarette butts, she would sit back and declare victory.

My father had a hi-fi stereo system that he'd built himself from various components. These were the days of vinyl, before CDs or streaming was even a fantastic dream in the minds of budding stereophiles like my father. He'd built a beautiful mahogany cabinet to house his components and amassed a large collection of albums. My father loved jazz and bluegrass, while my mother, a pianist, preferred classical music and opera. Puccini was, by far, her favorite.

Opera and classical music had not been in my father's repertoire when he met my mother, but she had trained him well. They bought a subscription to "The Met", the New York Metropolitan Opera, and traveled regularly to New York City to attend performances of Bohéme, Rigoletto, Pagliacci and others. Over the years my father became versed in the scores of all of them. Occasionally, when my father was away on business, my siblings and I took turns substituting as her date.

We steered clear of the living room on Sunday afternoons, preferring to give my parents their space while we hung out in the child friendly spaces of our two-story stucco on Preston Drive; the backyard, basement or attic bedrooms. But make no mistake, my parents' music could be heard from every corner of the house. Music on the hi-fi meant it was Sunday.

The music of Puccini served as the soundtrack for some of the most significant memories I had of my mother. As Jessica's voice filled the air around me, I slipped off again, into a distant memory, many years before. A memory I had long cherished of a time when my relationship with my mother was a simpler one.

I am upstairs in my bedroom, sick with a fever and home from school. I am wrapped in my pink denim bedspread, my head propped up on a pillow, a pile of Nancy Drew books beside me. My brothers and sister have already gone off to school. I hear the door close behind them and a rush of sadness comes over me.

The house is quiet. I hear my mother moving around on the floor below. Water running in the kitchen. The click of her footsteps on the tile floor.

At lunchtime she comes up to check on me. She has made some pastina in brodo, a chicken broth with small pasta stars that have settled to the bottom of the bowl. She has brought with her a recording of La Bohéme which she puts on my green plastic West-inghouse record player. As the music begins to play, she tells me the story of a pair of bohemian friends, Rudolfo and Marcello, who live in a garret in Paris.

She sits on the edge of the bed right next to me. "Marcello is a painter," my mother says, "And Rudolfo a poet. They are very poor. One day, after Marcello has gone off to meet their friends, Rudolfo meets Mimi, a neighbor, and the two fall in love."

My mother is a wonderful storyteller. She has begun writing a column for a local paper. She writes often about our family. Her stories are funny and tender, and she is never afraid to embellish.

"But there is not much money in being a poet," she says. "Rudolfo and Mimi are very poor. As winter comes and the snow falls outside, the attic where they live is very cold."

Bohéme is centered around the lives of two couples. Marcello and Musetta. Rudolfo and Mimi. My mother loved the character of Mimi. In the story, Mimi gets sick. The harsh realities of living a bohemian life in Paris in the 1800's takes its toll on her and she becomes deathly ill. In my memory I can hear my mother's voice. Feel the warmth of her body beside me. It is just the two of us, alone. It is rare to have my mother all to myself and although I am sick, at this moment I feel special.

Flash forward almost fifty years. This time it is my mother who is ill. I sit beside her, holding her hand and stroking her hair. The end is near. She is now seventy-nine years old and has been suffering with Alzheimer's disease for a long time. Like the Camino, the road we have traveled together has been a long one. It has not been easy.

Puccini plays on repeat in the background on a small CD player beside the bed. As the opening notes of Musetta's aria begin again, my mother, like Mimi, succumbs.

Now, three years later, there is nothing left but memories of her. I have done my work. In the years following her death I have examined my relationship with her and made peace with the pain that still lingered, even in those final moments.

As Jessica's voice fills the air, the outdoor dining room stills. An unexpected gift on a warm June night. As she sings the final note, a swell of applause takes its place. She smiles and glances sheepishly at her husband. The Italian couple from the albergue come up to the table to thank her. "Bravo," they say. "Bravo."

"Those were two of my mother's favorites," I said as we get ready to leave. I am suddenly overcome with emotion and I can feel the tears filling my eyes. "She died a few years ago after a long battle with Alzheimer's." I feel the need to explain. "Thank you," I whisper and reach out to give her a hug.

I walked back to the albergue, my head swimming in memories. I am surprised by how many times my thoughts have turned to my mother on the Camino. Each day, as I visited the churches along the way, I made sure to light two votives, one for her and one for my father. It was my mother who gave my siblings and me the gift of a love of travel. She took us to Europe for the first time when I was just a twelve-year-old girl and then again and again and still again. Over the years we'd visited most of the European countries and in the case of her beloved Italy, more than once.

We had family in Rome, the city where my maternal grandfather was raised. There were great aunts and uncles and cousins too. Each time we came to Europe we never missed an opportunity to visit them. To wander arm in arm like locals. To wind through the crazy Roman traffic in my uncle's Fiat or to sit at the large mahogany table and fill our bellies with Zia Bice's handmade pasta and freshly made crostata. Now, as I look back on those days, I understood that more than the opportunity to see the extraordinary architecture and art, those trips to Europe had given me something far more important, something I had taken for granted. An extraordinary connection to family. To a sense of history. To a culture that filled me with pride. A level of comfort no matter where I travelled. Europe felt like home.

Back at the albergue, my eye catches the shells that still hang from my pack. I'd begun the journey with three but lost one somewhere along the way. Curiously, it is the one with my own name inscribed inside. A metaphor, perhaps. The two that remain bear the names of my parents. For a moment I think back to our time together on Sanibel Island, where we'd spend hours combing the beach and filling our pockets with shells. Whelks. Coquinas. Spiny jewel boxes and cockles.

I'd meant the shells to be a reminder, a way to carry them with me, but I have found them all along this journey, without even looking, in places I never expected.

DAY 31
O'PEDROUZO
KILOMETER 760

CHAPTER 13

Thin Places

I stepped out from under the fluorescent lights of the albergue into the darkness of the early morning. The streetlights cast a soft glow on the stretch of empty sidewalks. The streets were quiet and for a time, I am alone. I was grateful for the silence. I feel a heaviness this morning, a sadness I had not expected. Tomorrow I will reach Santiago. I will reach the end of my Camino.

As I walk, images flicker in my memory as if flipping through a photo album. Scenes from the last 29 days flash across my consciousness. Random moments, filled with emotion. Listening to the church bells ring in Boadilla with Irish English John. Sharing a picnic lunch with the two young Irish medical students I call "The Camino docs". Savoring a glass of vino tinto and eating pimientos de padrón with Annabella in Triacastella. Moments spent laughing. Singing. Crying.

There'd been so many of them, these seemingly simple moments. Deceptive in their simplicity, they were so much more than they appeared to be. A multi-layered dimensionality. A kaleidoscope of expansiveness. Each time one happened I felt it deep inside. Like a gift I wanted to cling to, to savor, to hold close. Words betrayed me. I struggled to describe what I did not yet understand.

There was the afternoon in Hontanas. We walked 31 kilometers that first day on the meseta, past golden fields of wheat, large piles of rock and beneath a vibrant blue sky. We'd just checked into our albergue in an old 18th century building. We'd run through the usual routine. Taken showers. Done laundry. It was time for our afternoon caña, that mixture of beer and lemon soda I'd become so fond of. It was something we'd done plenty of times. It could have been any day. But it wasn't just any day,

Café tables spilled into the street. Debbie, Pat, Irish English John and I sat down together at one of the only tables that still had a few seats left. The air was electric with laughter and conversation. "Slainte," we said as we raised our glasses and toasted the day. It was an Irish toast we'd been using ever since the early days with Conor and Emma, and it served as a way of keeping them with us. Just then the bells of the church began to ring. *Clang. Clang. Clang. Clang.* A chill ran through my body. My heart pounded in my chest. I felt the desire to pinch myself. *This is incredible,* I thought. *Just a few weeks ago, none of us knew one another and now listen to sound of voices all around us.* I wondered if anyone else could *see* it. I wondered if anyone else could *feel* it.

That night a musician was performing across the street in a local bar. Marc and Martina were spreading the word. We'd just finished dinner and I was sitting outside, enjoying the cool evening air. "Come join us," they'd said. I gathered Debbie and Pat and we found our way across the street. In a dimly lit back room, away from the packed bar and the noisy street conversation, a woman played the guitar and sang. I bought a glass of wine and found an empty seat at the end of a long table. Marc, Martina and Raphael were there along with a handful of others, our attention trained on the singer.

She sat in the corner in front of a large fireplace, a string of twinkle lights sparkling behind her. She smiled as she sang, switching back and forth between Spanish and English in her bright soprano voice. She motioned us to sing along. We joined in on the chorus of the Camino anthem, *Ultreia,* a song we'd sung in Carrión de los Condes a few days earlier. We sang *Ring of Fire* by Johnny Cash and Billy Joel's *Piano Man*, but it was when she began Leonard Cohen's *Hallelujah* that I felt it. The way the room expanded when we sang in unison, *Hallelujah, Hallelujah, Hallelujah, Hallelujah*. The connections so visceral, the sense of something much bigger surrounding us. A holiness perhaps, and I wondered if the walls could even contain the joy.

There'd been that amazing rainbow in León, just after it stopped raining. My feet covered in blisters, I shuffled down the street feeling a profound sadness, fearful of the anticipated loneliness that was sure to come. I was wallowing in self-pity, already missing my friends who'd left early that morning. I poked my head into a small shop on the main street to get out of the rain, one of the few wet days we had on the Camino. I walked slowly through the shop, waiting for the skies to clear while I gazed at the glass cases filled with beautiful jewelry; silver, gold and sparkling gemstones. Along the far wall was a display of stretch bracelets made of small polished stone beads, each one with a little silver shell dangling from it. A souvenir of the Camino de Santiago. I bought one and stretched it onto my wrist.

By then the rain had stopped and I made my way out onto the street again, walking up towards the main square. And that's when I saw it, a rainbow in the direction of the cathedral, a prism stretched across the sky. When I saw it it stopped me in my tracks. My chest swelled and tears formed in the corners of my eyes and for a moment it took my breath away. I felt a lightness inside, as if I'd been given a sign. A promise that things were going to be OK. Inside, something shifted. And then, as quickly as it appeared, it was gone.

And then there was the night in Barbadelo, a tiny hamlet with not much more to it than a couple of albergues. I'd taken the long route that day in order to see the monastery at Samos, walking the 29. 5 kilometers (17.7 miles) with a couple of young women I'd met from Barcelona. I was feeling proud of myself having spent most of the day speaking Spanish. We'd parted ways just outside of Sarria and I continued on alone. By the time I finished the final 5 kilometers to Barbadelo, I was exhausted. I found a room in a small private albergue, took a shower and wandered out to find something to eat.

There was only one restaurant in town, so I found a table and ordered myself a glass of tinto de verano and a bite to eat. At the table next to me was a young man, sitting alone.

"Hi," I said. "Buen Camino."

"To you too. American?" he asked. "My name's Cameron."

I nodded. "Suzanne. Where are you from?"

"Capetown," he said. "South Africa."

"What? You're from Capetown?" A table away, two women were sitting together eating dinner.

"I am," he said.

"So are we," they said. "Come join us." We picked up our plates and glasses of wine and tucked in around the table for four.

The women were fraternal twins who now lived in London. They had a sharp wit about them and within seconds the conversation exploded into a raucous laugh-fest. The sisters played off each other, and Cameron joined in as if he'd known them forever. I refilled my wine glass and settled in for the ride. I felt like I'd gotten a front row seat at a local comedy club. Before long the sides of my face hurt from laughing. We promised to meet in the morning for breakfast.

I walked back down the street to my albergue, the moon just starting to come up. I called my son Dylan to wish him a happy birthday. We spoke for an hour or so and after I hung up, I began to get ready for bed. Just as I turned out the light, I heard a man's voice outside my second-floor window. I opened it and peeked my head out.

The tiny country lane was dark. A still silence permeated the air. From my window I could see a single lightbulb perched atop an old white barn just across the narrow dirt lane. The door to the barn was open, and a man stood under the light, calling into the darkness. Within minutes a cow appeared and walked past him into the barn. He called again, this time a different word, and another cow arrived. And another and another and still another. Each time the man called, another cow appeared and he swatted them gently on the behind as they found their way into the barn. And that's when I realized. He was calling them by name. Beckoning them home. I was mesmerized. It was a slow process, a beautiful process. One after the other they returned, like children who had been out to play.

There'd been so many moments like that along the way. Moments of simple grandeur that seemed to diminish the minute you tried to put words to them. Moments of purity. Of energy. Of light. Ever since the conversation with Robert about the Ignatian Spiritual practices, I'd been thinking about how to recognize the presence of God. Rather than think of God as something out there, an old man sitting on a puffy white cloud, I wondered how I might recognize those moments of holiness. To see God in my day-to-day life. Perhaps I'd taken them for granted.

There'd been a time when I found comfort in the traditions I'd known my whole life, like putting on a favorite sweater on a cold winter day, but that wasn't enough for me anymore. I was looking for more than comfort. I wanted to be inspired, moved in a way I had not felt in a very long time. I believed, of that I was certain. Whatever one called it, God, a higher power, the divine, an energy, I knew there was something greater than all of us. There had to be. But despite believing, I longed to close the distance that I could not seem to bridge.

Although many do, I did not set out to walk the Camino as a religious pilgrimage. Nor did I walk with the intention of exploring my faith, in search of answers to my questions let alone my relationship with God. But the more I walked, the more these questions presented themselves to me. Again and again, until I could no longer ignore them. Although I did not know it at the time, I *was* searching for something. A deepening of understanding. A sense of connection.

There is a concept in Celtic Christianity known as a Thin Place. It is a place where, as Rev. Dr. Mark Roberts explains, "the boundary between heaven and earth is especially thin. It's a place where we can sense the divine more readily." Maybe, this was what I was searching for, a way to experience the divine. It wasn't enough to "know" it, I needed to feel it. To be in it. I needed to find my thin place.

Sunlight sparkled through the trees above me while I walked along the path this morning. Tears flowed freely down my face as I contemplated the ending of my journey. Tears had become a regular occurrence in recent days. I did not wipe them away. It felt good to cry, to let the emotion out. I passed a hedge of multicolored hydrangea, purples and blues and bright pinks. Everything seemed more vibrant than usual today, or maybe I was just paying closer attention. I inhaled deeply, trying to commit this moment to memory. I stepped through an opening in the hedgerow to find a small, outdoor café with a cluster of picnic tables for seating. Three pilgrims, a man and two women, each sitting at separate tables, sipped coffee and ate empanadas, another specialty of this region of Galicia.

"Buen Camino," the man says as I enter and I begin to sob, deep heaving sobs where I can't catch my breath, as though I am crying from the very bottom of my soul. He jumps up, wraps his arms around me in a big bear hug, and holds me tight. "It's going to be OK," he says. "It's all going to be OK."

I lean into him, the combined weight of my body and my backpack seeming to melt into his embrace. "Is it?" I asked. I wasn't so sure.

"Sit down," he says. "Join us for a while." He smiled broadly and I recognized his South African accent immediately.

I slid my pack off and began to wipe the tears from my eyes. I inhaled deeply, filling my chest with the warmth of the morning air. I felt embarrassed by my sudden burst of emotion in front of these people I haven't even met yet. "I'm Suzanne," I say, addressing the group. "I'm sorry about that. I've been crying all morning. I'm just so sad that it's almost over."

"It's OK," one of the women says. She is sitting alone at the edge of the table just to the right of the South African. "We all understand."

I fish some money out of my pack and go inside. I order a café con leche and a slice of tuna empanada and then make my way back to a picnic table.

"May I join you?" I ask the other one. She too has her own table and I motion to the seat next to her.

"Of course. My name is Alessandra." I recognize their accents right away. One Dutch, the other Italian.

"Where are you from in Italy?" I ask.

"Napoli," she says.

"Ah, my family lives in Roma." My voice trembles as I speak and the tears begin to flow again. I take a sip of my coffee and slice off a piece of empanada. I am out of sync. My outside does not reflect what is going on inside. Inside I am crumbling. I feel vulnerable, like a little girl.

The South African sits atop his picnic table, his broad body filling the space. He reaches into his pocket and pulls out a cigarette. I have been alone all morning with my thoughts. I am grateful to have found them, to have someone to share this moment with.

"This has been the most amazing experience," I say, "Unlike anything I've ever done. I don't even know how to explain it."

The woman from Holland looks at me. "I know exactly what you mean. I don't want it to end. And I'm worried, you know? Because I don't think anyone who hasn't done this can understand."

"It's not at all what I thought it was going to be. I mean, before I came, I did what I could to get ready. I spent all that time preparing to walk, going for hikes with friends. Getting all the right equipment. But the funny thing is, none of it really mattered. You can't really prepare for something like this. The thing is, it isn't really about the walk, is it?"

"I know. I've been struggling to explain it to my husband. He's with me. Not on the walk, but he's traveling along, staying in a camper. Most of the time I'm spending my nights in alber-gues, but every couple of days I join him for a night, but each time I do, I can't wait to get back. It feels like I'm straddling two worlds."

I knew exactly what she meant. I'd been feeling it for days now. This sense of being in some kind of alternate place, dis-connected from normal life, or at least what I considered to be normal. And yet, at the same time, even in the disconnect, I felt more connected. More present. More alive. I couldn't quite put my finger on it, couldn't find the words to describe what I was feeling, but in this moment it didn't seem to matter. Even without words, I knew they understood.

Perhaps I had found my thin place.

We sat and talked for a long while, the Italian, the woman from Holland, the South African and I. Long after the empanadas and coffee were gone and the air around us warmed by the strength of the midday sun. We talked about what came next. How we might feel once we reached Santiago. We wondered how to hold on to the feeling we had. That sense of connection. To each other and to the journey. The calmness. The clarity. The knowledge about what really mattered.

The next day we would walk into Santiago. In the days ahead we would return to the lives we'd left behind. What would happen when we returned home? Would we slip back into the familiar? Far away from the calm of The Way, would we get sucked back into the chaos? We didn't want to. As we sat there and reminisced about the days since we'd left St-Jean-Pied-de-Port, we tried to put words to something we struggled to explain. In the miles between here and there, we'd discovered something, although none of us knew for certain what it was. We just knew it to be true.

DAY 32
SANTIAGO
KILOMETER 779

CHAPTER 14

Windows

I folded into the steady stream of pilgrims walking into town. We wound our way through traffic circles, past a handful of markers decorated with stones and shells and talismans left by the hundreds or perhaps thousands who had walked these same steps. For the first time since I'd left St-Jean-Pied-de-Port, I did not pay attention to the birds singing or notice the flowering cactus or smell the scotch broom. My thoughts not lost in a sea of memories. Instead, I followed along mindlessly, quickening my pace as I moved in the direction of the cathedral. Like a wave coming to rest on the shore, I was focused on the destination.

The text from my husband that morning had been one of congratulations. "You're almost there,' he'd said. "Enjoy the final few kilometers today. Let us know when you get to Santiago. We are so very proud of you."

I'd been so surprised when the first few texts came. So moved by his support along the way. He'd not missed a day since I'd begun walking. Bob was a quiet man. A man of few words. He'd never been overly demonstrative and unlike me, he didn't wear his heart on his sleeve. His messages had been filled with kind words and inspirational pictures, each one different than the last.

The final 12 kilometers went quickly. I walked through the new part of town, past stores and office buildings, squished onto concrete sidewalks as the long flow of pilgrims snaked their way through the busy streets of Santiago. Cars whizzed by, a montage of newness in stark contrast to the history we'd spent that past month wandering though. Despite being surrounded by dozens of pilgrims taking these final steps together, I felt oddly alone.

As the line of pilgrims meandered through the streets like a school of fish swimming together, I found myself next to a couple of young women from England. We chatted for a few minutes as we walked. They'd begun their journey in Sarria, just a hundred kilometers out. I'd come the whole way, I'd said. They seemed impressed, and for the first time since I began walking, I felt truly proud of what I'd accomplished. And then, when we reached the gate to the old city, the Porta Real, the energy changed. The pace quickened. We were almost there.

The nasal sounds of a bagpipe reverberated off the stone buildings in a welcome to Santiago that marked our arrival. A small crowd gathered in the archway just outside the cathedral square. I walked clumsily, tripping on the uneven cobbled streets and feeling the weight of my tired feet against the stone steps. I stepped out into the Praza do Obradoiro, the grand plaza in front of the cathedral of Santiago. The size of the square startled me. It was enormous, one of the biggest ones I'd ever seen and the few groups of pilgrims that congregated in various corners of the square seemed insignificant in the shadow of the towering stone cathedral. The sky was a cobalt blue, peppered with tiny puffs of white. The twin spires of the massive church stretched triumphant against the summer sky. I asked one of the two British women to take my photo as I raised my arms in triumph. I returned the favor and then sent the picture off to my husband. I made it.

I stood in the center of the square and gazed at the cathedral. After 32 days on the Camino, I wasn't sure how to feel. Elated? Thrilled? Accomplished? At this exact moment, none of those things came to mind. Instead, I felt numb and although I wasn't sure what I expected, it certainly wasn't this. I looked around, hoping to see a familiar face, someone to acknowledge the moment, but there were none to be found.

Pilgrims continued to enter the square in a steady stream. I scanned their faces and watched as the scene repeated itself again and again. Hands raised in the air in triumph. A flurry of hugs in celebration. But there had been no one for me to hug. No one to share this most profound moment of accomplishment. My journey had ended the way it began.

The longer I stood there, the more I began to feel overwhelmed. It was all too much. The hordes of people, the expanse of the square, the feeling of emptiness. For the past 31 days I had a purpose. A goal. I knew what I had to do. Now, for the first time in a month, it wasn't clear. There was nowhere left to go.

The pilgrim Mass, a ritual of arrival in Santiago, would be starting at noon. I'd looked forward to seeing the Botafumeiro.

One of the largest in the world, it was the thurible of incense that hung from the ceiling of the cathedral. The ceremonial swinging of the Botafumeiro was legendary, the incense pouring from the cavity as it traversed the expanse of the cathedral. But it was not to be. The cathedral was closed for renovations and scaffolding covered every square inch of the inside. Instead, Mass would be at the nearby Iglesia de San Francisco, right next door to my hotel.

I checked my watch. There was still enough time to get my Compostela, so I made my way down to the pilgrim office. Inside, the line stretched down the long hallway. Thirty minutes later I presented both *credenciales* to the woman at the desk. I'd collected so many stamps that I'd needed to get a second one in León and now that one was almost full too. She looked at them, noting the starting point in St-Jean-Pied-de-Port.

"You have come a long way," she said. "Congratulations."

"I have," I smiled. I'd walked the whole thing. Every single step. All 779 kilometers of them.

As I came to the final days of the Camino, I began to think about continuing on to Finesterre, a small fishing village on the coast. The name came from the Roman *fines terrae*, meaning the end of the earth. While most people finished their walk in Santiago, I kind of liked the idea of going as far as one could go, to the westernmost point of Spain. It wasn't that much further, just another 3-day walk. Irish English John planned to go the rest of the way and I decided to go with him.

"Wait for me to walk to Finisterre." I'd said in a text a few days earlier.

"OK," he'd texted back. "It will be good to have a friend to walk with."

It had been almost two weeks since we'd parted ways in León and I missed him. In the first two weeks of the Camino there'd been hardly a day when we didn't walk together at least part of the time. Other than Debbie and Pat, Irish English John had been my most steady companion on that first part of the journey, someone I'd looked forward to catching up with each day. I missed sharing a pint or two after a long day's walk, and I was looking forward to having one more chance to do it all again.

But by the time I got to Santiago, he was gone. "Where are you?" I asked as I stood in line, waiting to receive my Compostela.

"I'm on my way to Finisterre," he said. "I got to Santiago early and just needed to keep going. I never planned to finish my Camino there anyway."

I stared blankly at my phone for a few seconds, unsure of what to do next. Once again, as I had in León, I felt hurt. Disappointed. His leaving surprised me. Hadn't he realized I'd been looking forward to finishing this journey together? Didn't he know how important it was to me? Was there something else I wasn't aware of? Something I didn't understand?

The relationships I'd built on this journey had become very important to me. They were family and I was committed to them, to the path we'd taken together and the friendships we'd developed. But for me, those relationships came with expectations. Expectations that often lead to disappointment because they often went unmet. Rather than appreciate what I had, I would long for what I wanted.

I expected Irish English John to wait. I hoped he'd want to wait. And when he didn't, I found myself struggling to make sense of something I did not yet understand. I had my own views about the way things should be. My own beliefs about family. About relationship. About friendship. I was struck by how my expectations got in my way and kept me from appreciating and accepting what was, rather than what might be. It wasn't fair. To him or to me. And yet, despite being given that lesson over and over again, it was something I still needed to work on.

All of a sudden my plans had changed. Compostela in hand, I trudged back up the stone steps into the square, wondering what to do next.

"Suzanne. You made it!" I turned to see a familiar face coming towards me.

Alex was from Hamburg. I'd met him on day 5, somewhere between Puente La Reina and Estella. He was handsome, fair-skinned, blue eyed and about 10 years younger than me. Although he kept apologizing for it, his English was good enough to spend the kilometers talking about all sorts of things, from family to politics to the German system of government. I told him I'd been to Munich and Stuttgart as a young girl. I'd even spent a birthday in Heidelberg. Germany was a place my father loved. My thoughts turned to an old photo from one of those trips, my siblings and me sitting at a table in Munich's Hofbrauhaus while my father hoisted a mug of German beer into the air. I was struck how often that happened along the Camino. When meeting a person or hearing a story takes you back into your memory, as if each person was a window into yourself.

Those early days were hot. I was still finding my way, still struggling with sore feet, carrying a 20-pound pack and remembering to drink enough water. I was carrying a liter water bottle in an outside pocket of my pack, but I couldn't reach it without stopping to take the whole thing off. It was the only flaw I'd found with the pack I'd chosen. It took just a few stops along the way before Alex started to hand me my water, replacing it after I'd finished. Soon I began to feel guilty. If he handed me water once, he'd done it more than a dozen times. But Alex never complained. He was far too kind for that. The sun beat down on us and there was little shade. On the second day of walking together, I ran out of water. Alex kept me going by sharing his.

We'd lost track of each other somewhere after Logroño. I'd heard through the Camino grapevine that he too had problems with blisters, but I hadn't heard much more than that. I figured he'd be like so many of the others I'd met along the way. Someone who'd be a part of my Camino for just a few days and then slip away, leaving little more than a memory behind, but here he was.

Alex stretched out his arms and wrapped me up in a big bear hug.

"You're still here," I said. I leaned into him, wrapping my arms tightly around him. I'd heard that he was leaving early that morning to go back to Hamburg.

"I couldn't leave without saying goodbye," he said as we hugged. "I couldn't leave without saying goodbye to my dear friend."

As I looked back on my journey, I began to realize that the Camino was a little like putting together a jigsaw puzzle, one in which the pieces were all fragments of me. Of the life I'd lived. The people I'd loved. The pain I'd carried. The dreams I'd held. In each moment there was always something to be found. In a warm smile or a shared meal. In the embrace of an encouraging word on a hard day or after a long talk on the meseta there was always a treasure to mine. A memory. A remembrance. A moment long ago.

I thought of a favorite quote from the mindfulness teacher Jon Kabat Zinn, "Wherever you go, there you are." It was the thing I loved the most, the thing I was most grateful for. The ability to connect with others and see yourself reflected in that connection. The opportunity to learn about others and about oneself. We were all walking the same path. Putting one foot in front of the other. Doing the best we could. That was the gift of human connection.

I'd come to understand that the Camino wasn't just about the walk. It was about what happened *while* we were walking. It was about noticing the sunshine and the storks. The bright red poppies and the rows of tempranillo grapes. It was about tasting the café con leche and the midmorning tortilla. The ice-cold beers and lukewarm showers.

But for me, the Camino was mostly about the people. The dozens I met and the thousands I would never meet. It was about slowing down enough to listen. About looking into someone's eyes and seeing their heart. It was about what could happen when we peeled away the layers of noise and distraction in our lives, the insulation that keeps us from truly connecting. It was about reaching out and touching others. It was about letting down your guard and allowing yourself to be touched. The Camino was about connection. The opportunities were there. All it took was for us to notice.

I watched Alex walk across the square, turning to wave one more time before he disappeared into the crowd. Tears streamed down my face as I watched him leave. A cocktail of sadness and grief, joy and gratitude all jumbled into one. It would be the first of many goodbyes in the next few days and I knew it wasn't going to get any easier.

I went off to find my hotel. I would take a shower and then head over to the pilgrim Mass. I'd made a reservation at the San Francisco Hotel Monumento, a luxury by any stretch of the imagination, especially after all the nights spent in bunk beds over the past month. I took a hot shower, wrapped myself in fluffy white towels and lay across the bed. My body felt heavy. The muscles in my legs twitched. I breathed deeply, noticing the rise and fall of my chest and soon I felt myself surrender. For the first time since I'd begun walking I was being forced to acknowledge what I hadn't wanted to admit. I was tired.

I woke up about 30 minutes later, cold and damp and too late for the pilgrim Mass. I'd have to go tomorrow. I got dressed, sent a text to Pat and Debbie, finalizing our arrangement to meet up for a drink and then I found my way back to the square.

Now, the square was full of people. Amidist the sea of bodies, I spotted them immediately. They were sitting on the bench that ran the length of the cement wall on the west side of the square. They looked relaxed. Refreshed even. I waved frantically and bounded my way towards them. "Hi," I said, as I wrapped my arms around Debbie and then Pat. "We made it!" It had been ten days since I'd left them early that morning in Astorga. I'd missed them and although we'd stayed in touch by text, I was happy to be with them again.

We grabbed a table at the outdoor café at the Parador Hotel and ordered two glasses of tinto de verano and an icy cold beer. I couldn't wait to catch up and hear how they'd been since we'd been apart.

From Astorga they'd taken a bus up to the iron cross at Foncebadón, and then made their way by foot from there. "How'd you guys do on O'Cebreiro?" I asked. "The climb wasn't as bad as I thought it was going to be, or maybe we're just in better shape."

"We went over it on horseback," Debbie said. "There was a place in Herrerías where you could rent them. We went up with a group. It was really fun."

I laughed. "That would have been awesome." I said. "I love riding horses. Was it scary at all?"

"No, the horses were really surefooted," said Pat. "You got the sense that they've done it a lot. They knew exactly where to go."

We picked up where we'd left off. It was strange, in the ten days since I'd last seen them, we'd each had our own adventures, but our connections to each other were cemented from the moment we'd first met back in St-Jean.

"I see you have your bracelet on," I said to Debbie, raising my wrist to display my own. I slid my arm over next to hers.

"Camino twins," she said. "I'm never going to take it off."

The next morning I woke up and mechanically checked my phone, expecting to see a text from Bob. It was something I'd done every day since that first morning in St-Jean-Pied-de-Port. But to my disappointment, there was nothing there, a harsh reminder that my journey was really over. It was at that moment that I realized just how much his messages had meant to me. How much I'd looked forward to receiving them. They had buoyed me each day, sending me off on the day's walk with a piece of home that sustained me more than he knew. More than that, they'd made me feel truly seen.

I ran into Marc later that afternoon. It was the Fourth of July, but more importantly, it was his birthday.

"Happy birthday," I shouted, stretching my arms out to swallow him in an enthusiastic embrace.

"Let's have dinner together," he said, "Peggy's still around and she wants to join us."

"I'd love to celebrate with you and Peggy," I said, my voice teeming with excitement. "I'm so glad she made it."

In the days after I'd wrapped Peggy's knee in the ace bandage, I made sure to check in with her to see how she was feeling when I passed her along the way. "Better," she always seemed to say. Although she was moving slowly, she'd continued to walk but it had been more than a few days since I'd last seen her. I hoped she'd been able to finish. We planned to meet for tapas later that evening.

Peggy greeted each of us with a big hug, her face beaming. We sat down at an outdoor table and ordered some traditional tortilla, garlic sauteed mushrooms and, on my insistence, a plate of Pulpo a la Gallega. We raised glasses of wine and toasted our time together.

"You two are my heroes," Peggy said.

I smiled at her quizzically. "Heroes?" I asked. I wasn't sure what she was talking about.

"You saved me," she answered. "I will never forget that."

I thought back to the day she'd hobbled into the rest area, her eyes filled with tears. She was hurting and I reached out to help. Just a single moment in a month full of moments. It could have been anyone. I just happened to be there. I knew she'd appreciated my help. She'd told me that at the time, but now I was surprised to hear how much it had meant to her. How my actions had impacted her journey.

As we sat there together, sharing stories and finishing every single piece of the pulpo, I found myself breathing in the moment, trying to capture what would soon be just a memory. Peggy would be returning to Hong Kong in the morning and Marc would be leaving to walk to Finisterre. As I sat across from them, I considered the randomness of it all. Here we were, strangers from different parts of the world who might never have met but for a common desire to walk the Camino. How lucky we were.

Before I left to walk the Camino I'd read *The Pilgrimage*, by Paolo Coelho. An allegorical tale, it tells the story of Coelho's own journey to Santiago. In it, the narrator meets a handful of colorful characters that teach him about love. At the time that I read it, I hadn't understood. But one day, as I was walking along, something clicked. I don't remember where I was, but I don't suppose it matters. All of a sudden the story came back to me. Like Coelho, I'd met my own set of colorful characters along the way, but it would take me a while to understand the lessons they had to teach me.

The next afternoon I took the bus to Finesterre. It was the first time I'd been in a vehicle in over a month. I watched the scenery speed by, so fast I barely noticed what I was seeing. *This is what my life was like,* I thought. *Moments speeding by without taking the time to notice. Days that passed too quickly. A focus on getting somewhere rather than the journey itself. How much I'd missed. How little I'd paid attention.* Walking had taught me to slow down. To pay attention. To see more clearly. Now, as I contemplated returning to the life I'd left behind, I wondered if it was possible to do things differently. To continue to walk once I got home.

After the bus dropped us off, I went off to find my hotel, a lovely place at the top of a hill with a beautiful view of the ocean. It was getting late in the day and I was anxious to begin walking again so I dropped off my bag and made my way back down the hill.

The trail hugged the coastline, past the old Castelo de San Carlos at the edge of town to the lighthouse at the point. The ocean to the left of us was a reminder of just how far we'd come. Along the way I ran into Sarah and Elizabeth, two women I'd met at the top of O'Cebreiro where we'd shared a plate of fresh bread and queso y miel. We continued on together, making quick time of the 6.4 kilometer walk to the point. Words spilled into the spaces between us as we struggled to process this extraordinary journey. We passed the 0.0 marker and stopped to take a picture. Ahead of us stood the lighthouse, the place that was once believed to be the end of the world.

I walked out beyond the lighthouse and found a seat on a large outcropping of rocks that overlooked the sea. A thick band of clouds hugged the horizon, blurring the boundary between sea and sky. There was nowhere left to go. I closed my eyes and felt the warmth of the sun on the rocks and the crisp ocean breeze on my face. Emotions bubbled up faster than I could process them. I was tired but also invigorated. Overwhelmed and yet somehow content. My heart broke at the realization that my journey was over, but at the same time, so filled with gratitude that it felt like it was going to burst. Unable to control the sea of emotion, I let it wash over me. It would be a long time before I'd be able to make sense of what I'd just been through.

The next morning I walked down to the ocean one last time. The sun was shining and the sea was calm. I took off my shoes and socks and stood in the water, watching the sand wrap around my blistered feet. Small air bubbles rose to the surface as the waves lapped against me. I reached down to pick up a couple of razor clam shells and a large pink scallop shell and tucked them into my pocket. I'd come to the end of my journey. In the morning I would be heading back to Barcelona to spend a few days with a friend and then fly home. I made plans to have dinner with, Debbie, Pat, Patrick and Maria, the last remaining members of our original Camino family.

Back in Santiago, it was an afternoon of goodbyes. I meandered through the streets stumbling upon many of the people I'd walked with over the past four weeks. We hugged and took selfies and shared a laugh and a memory. The Dutch guy who'd walked all the way from his home in Holland. Like me, he too was about to turn 60. His walk had taken 100 days, but he made it, arriving one day before his 60th birthday. In the market I saw the playful Polish couple Irish English John and I'd had dinner with one night. "Ameri-can," he'd called when he saw me on the trail. Neither one of them spoke English, at least not enough to have a conversation, but that never stopped us. Somehow we'd managed. While we spoke in English and he in Polish, a lot was accomplished with an array of hand motions, broad smiles and a whole bunch of laughter.

"Ameri-can, Ameri-can," he yelled when he saw me, waving me over. He stood at a nearby counter where a cheese monger held a hunk of pale-yellow cheese in the air. "Probst," he seemed to say, putting his fingers to his mouth, "Probst."

She cut off a piece of the gorgeous cheese, a creamy, nutty slice of deliciousness. The Polish guy smiled broadly and then proceeded to tell me God knows what with an exhilaration that was contagious. He offered me some cherries and then wrapped me up in a big hug before he and his wife disappeared into the crowd. I would miss them. They were effervescent, like sparkling wine on a bright summer's day.

We ran into Smitha, the writer from India, on the way back from dinner. Our paths had crossed many times over the miles. Like me, she'd been one of the ones who'd had her things stolen that first night in Roncesvalles. We'd explored a church museum and searched for carved skulls together in Castrojeriz. She was quiet and reflective and like me, shared a fascination with the extraordinary art that seemed to be almost everywhere you looked.

Around every corner was another familiar face. That night in León when my feet were blistered so badly that I could barely walk, I'd been so disappointed when my friends walked on without me. Worried that I would be alone. Afraid to trust the path forward, I clung to what I already knew. It was a pattern that was all too familiar. I'd done it many times before.

But I had been wrong. I could not know that in the days ahead I would meet Benny. Or the South Africans or so many others. You see, the thing I didn't know was that the Camino is one big family. We were all walking together, finding our own way. In taking that extra day of rest in León, I hadn't lost my family, I'd expanded it. Like the roads I had not yet walked, there were new people to meet, new stories to hear, new memories to create.

My Camino was over. In the past 32 days I'd walked 779 kilometers, almost 500 miles. And yet, as I looked back, it seemed to have passed in the blink of an eye. Now, as I thought back on the journey, the days seemed to run together. I could not distinguish one town from the next. Although I was tired, my body reverberated with an electricity I had not felt in a very long time. Still, one question remained. Despite the countless times I'd been asked, I still did not know why I'd walked. What it was that had called me to make this journey.

It would be many months before the answer would become clear. Long after I'd returned home to step back into the life that I'd left to begin my journey. The death of my parents had indeed been a reminder of the transience of life. And turning 60 a catalyst for action. Although I did not know it, I needed a reset, a chance to step away to listen to what I could not hear amidst the noise of everyday life. To step into the unknown in order to see what I could not see. To ask the questions I didn't even know to ask. To learn what I needed to learn and be reminded of what I already knew.

The Camino reminded me that connection is the thing that matters most to me, the chance to build deep and meaningful relationships with the people in my life. Of how important it is to bear witness to the journeys of others. How necessary it is to be aware of our own expectations and to recognize that, sometimes, those same expectations can get in the way of truly being present.

I was reminded that I have always needed to be a part of something bigger than myself because that is what gives my life meaning. That I am happiest when I strive to bring light to others because that's how I find my way through the darkness.

I learned that, for me, God is not found in religious traditions, rote prayers or ornate cathedrals. It is in relationship that I find God. That is where my spirituality lies. In reaching out a hand to others. In opening my heart to their stories. In recognizing that we are all part of the same family.

Of course, some of these illuminations were not new to me, but the time on the Camino allowed me the opportunity to reflect, to remind myself what really mattered and recommit to living these values as I continue on this journey we call life. As I walked along, I was struck by the gift that each person was, a separate star that illuminated my very being. A light that I would carry forward when I returned home and as I faced the inevitable moments of darkness that would come in the days ahead. The light that would help me remember who I truly was.

The streets were crowded as I walked back towards the square. The night sky cast a bluish light on the old stone buildings. My heart was full of more emotion that I could sort through in the moment. I felt dizzy as the noise of conversation and the celebrations swirled around me. I looked down at my feet as if trying to feel the ground beneath me and anchor myself in the moment. And then, when I looked up, there he was. Benny.

I was so glad to see him. After walking together during the most difficult days of the journey, we'd parted ways eight days before. We kept in touch since then, checking in at least once a day. Benny began the Camino with his daughter, but the two had separated somewhere along the way. In Villafranca, Benny waited for his daughter to catch up, and then the two of them finished the journey together, arriving that afternoon. When I'd last seen him he was moving slowly, his knees and blisters getting the better of him. But now, as he stood in front of me, he looked refreshed and invigorated.

I was struck by how different he seemed from the man I'd left eight days before. He was a handsome man, with a thick head of gray hair, a neatly kept goatee and a smile that stretched from ear to ear. Benny's warmth shone like a light in his eyes. He reached out to hug me. "I've been looking for you," he said. "I couldn't leave without saying thank you. I'd never have made it if it wasn't for you. I wanted to give up, but you kept me going."

I wrapped my arms around him as we celebrated together. "I always knew you would make it," I said, "And here you are." I thought back to the guilt I felt when I'd walked on without him. In those difficult miles when it hurt just to take a step, Benny had been there for me. And while I'd been there for him, I was disappointed by my lack of patience and compassion, frustrated by my limitations. I'd imagined he'd been upset with me. After all, hadn't I been letdown when my friends walked on without me? And yet, if that were true, you would never have known it from the way he greeted me now.

We chatted for a few minutes, catching up on his arrival to Santiago. After a while I said goodbye and walked back to the plaza. I would be leaving early in the morning and I wanted to see the cathedral one more time. I gazed up at the towering greyed stone façade, a striking contrast to the blackness of the night sky. I wasn't sure I was ready to leave and yet I didn't want to stay. Things already felt different. In the three days I'd been in Santiago, the magic of the past month began to fade. The delight in each new day. The anticipation of what came next. The joy I felt spending time with my newfound friends. Like a photograph whose edges begin to tear while the color slowly seeps from the frame, it was already beginning to feel like a dream. I wondered what came next. How would I hold on to the magic that was my Camino? The joy of discovery? The wonder of each new day? When I returned home, how would I carry the Camino spirit with me?

Epilogue

Onward

I began planning my next Camino even before I unpacked from
my first. I would return the following year to do the Camino
del Norte. The route begins near the French border in the town
of Irún and travels 824 kilometers across the Spanish coastline to Arzúa where it turns inward to make the final descent
into Santiago. Or maybe I would do the Camino Portugues,
the path that begins in southern Portugal in the city of Lisbon
and travels north, reaching Santiago in a mere 622 kilometers.
Somehow, knowing I'd be returning the following year made
the transition to post Camino life a little easier.

When I left Santiago, I spent a few more days in Barcelona with an old friend and then flew to the south of France
to spend a few days with my brother Robert and his family on
their vacation before returning home. I bought an inexpensive
swimsuit and a sundress at an outdoor market in Barcelona.
That combined with my now tired Camino clothes would be
enough to get me through. My feet still showed the effects of

the 779 kilometers I'd just walked. Although they no longer caused me pain, I still had blisters on both heels and the balls of my feet had lost several layers of skin. In addition, I lost a toenail on my right foot. Something I hoped would grow back given some time.

My brother picked me up at the train station in Nice and we drove to St. Tropez, a beautiful seaside town where the sun sparkled on red tile roofs and sprays of candy pink bougainvillea spilled over the walls of cream-colored buildings. I rented a small studio apartment and walked into town each morning to grab a freshly baked chocolate croissant and a café au lait before meeting my brother and his family for a day on the beach. I read and napped and soaked up the sun and drank far too many glasses of French rosé. At night, after a delicious dinner and with the evening still thick with the heat of the day, I would open the doors to the small second story patio, turn on the fan and fall fast asleep.

Still, as lovely as it sounds, I found myself struggling with the sharp contrast in environments. That small studio apartment without air conditioning cost almost as much for three days as my entire Camino altogether. While the café and croissant I had each morning was delicious, I was shocked by the 10 euro check that came along with it. On the Camino, 10 euro was enough to buy an entire dinner complete with a carafe of house wine. "Toto," I said repeating the line Dorothy speaks to her dog in the Wizard of Oz, " I have a feeling we're not in Kansas anymore."

But it wasn't just about the money. I wrestled with the opulence. The café overlooked a harbor lined with multimillion-dollar yachts, each with their own staff. The shop windows were filled with lavish fabrics and jewel bedecked garments. Handmade leather purses hung on the arms of well-appointed mannequins and beautiful French linens lined the boutique shelves.

I do not mean to sound critical or judgmental. It was an extraordinarily beautiful place. The warm sunshine and sandy beaches were a lovely respite for my feet to heal. And as I celebrated my birthday with my brother and his family at an outdoor restaurant eating wood-fired pizza and drinking French rosé under a magnificent canopy of flowers, I felt grateful. It was hard to imagine a better place to begin my 60th year than with some of the people I loved the most in the world. Still, after spending more than a month on the Camino, I found myself confronted with the inherent contradiction of the worlds I was straddling.

I'd grown accustomed to the simplicity of the Camino. The singular focus of each day. The slowness of pace. The meditative movements. The warmth of the people. The sense of calm I'd felt. Now, as I walked into town, cars buzzed by. Waiters rushed between tables without making eye contact. People pushed past me on the street. There was an urgency in the air I had not felt in a while.

I returned home a few days later to another birthday celebration. Bob planned a wonderful outdoor gathering complete with a musical performance of songs he and his friends had practiced while I was gone. I spent most of the afternoon sharing pictures and stories from my trip. I tried as best I could to introduce my friends to some of the people I'd met as I relayed tales from the month-long journey. But the more I tried to translate the experiences, the more I found my words inadequate. The stories rang hollow. The two-dimensionality of my photographs could not convey the depth of the moment. As much as I tried, I couldn't seem to capture what I'd been through. Despite their smiles and nods of acknowledgment, I couldn't help thinking they didn't really understand. It was as if I was in possession of something the others were not, although what, I was still not sure.

As the months wore on, I stayed in touch with my Camino family through text and video calls. Smitha and I began to chat about returning to the Camino and discussing possible routes we might take. Maria came to the book launch for my memoir, *The Cardinal Club,* and brought her sister along. Annabella made plans to visit when she came to San Francisco on a business trip in the fall.

One day I got an email from Debbie. "How are you my Camino sister?" she said. "I think of you every morning when I put on my bracelet." After I bought the small polished stone bracelet in León, I'd run into Debbie and Pat on the street. I'd shown Debbie the bracelet and she rushed off to buy one too. We'd playfully dubbed ourselves 'Camino twins', as we flaunted our matching bracelets. Like Debbie, I still wore mine every day. "I miss you," she said.

"I miss you too," I answered.

I wondered if she knew how much she and Pat had meant to me. That first night in St-Jean-Pied-de-Port, when I mustered up enough courage to say hello for the first time, I could not imagine how much I would come to depend on them. We were a perfect match. They were steady and dependable, generous and kind. As the days wore on, we found a similar rhythm. We shared meals and lodging and hours of conversation. They shared their journey with me and each day, when I walked on ahead, I always knew they'd be there at the end of the day.

In October a series of wildfires raged through northern California that burned uncontained for several weeks. The air was thick with smoke, and it was difficult to breathe. School was canceled. Homes destroyed. I received a text from Irish English John early one morning.

"Just looking at the fire in the California wine region," It said. "I hope you aren't in that area."

"Actually, yes," I replied, "That's exactly where I live. Our house is fine but the communities to the north of us have all been evacuated. It's heartbreaking. Fire destroyed the same area just two years ago."

"It really brings it home when you know somebody near the danger," he said. "Keep safe."

It was true. Ever since the Camino, the world felt much smaller. I now watched the evening news with a different perspective. As the European Union and England negotiated the terms of Brexit, I wondered what the impact would be on my Irish and English friends. And then, in November, protests erupted in Hong Kong. I reached out to Peggy. I was worried about her.

"Hello my Camino friend," I said, "I hope you are well. I've been reading about the situation in Hong Kong and I can't help but think of you and hope that you are safe."

"Thanks," she replied. "I'm safe but Hong Kong is really in a critical situation. Thank you for always remembering me."

By late December, fires had erupted in Australia. "I am OK," Marc wrote when I texted him to check in. "I live in the suburbs of Melbourne, so thankfully the fires are far from here, but the smoke is very bad."

I knew a little something about living with all of that smoke. When the fires raged in northern California, the midday sky was filled with so much smoke that it appeared as if it were the middle of the night. Ash covered the cars and sidewalks. "Be careful," I said. "Wear a mask. The smoke in the air can be very dangerous."

And then in March the whole world came to a screeching halt. I had just finished teaching for the day when word came down from the local health department that the county where I live, as well as many of the others in our area, would be going to a shelter in place order. The deadly coronavirus pandemic that had been raging in other parts of the globe had now reached California. As had been true in places all over the world, there would be no more public gatherings. Restaurants closed. Businesses shuttered their doors. The pandemic brought life to a standstill.

While some of my friends lost their jobs, I was lucky. I transitioned to online teaching. While it wasn't ideal, at least I could continue to work. I could see the effects of the isolation my students felt long before I felt it myself. They began to tell me stories of loved ones who'd contracted the virus. Many struggled to adjust to new living situations, returning home after having a taste of the freedoms of living on their own. Cut off from social relationships, they began to express feelings of depression and anxiety. As odd as it might sound, I could feel their pain through the computer screen.

It was a strange juxtaposition to the journey I'd taken just the year before. When the road and days stretched out ahead of me without limitation. When a chance encounter along the way could lead to a new friendship and an afternoon of conversation. Now, there was nowhere to go. No chance encounters or journeys to unexpected places. I went days without leaving my house. Everything felt prescribed. Life became sanitized. A trip to the grocery store was a major ordeal. I began to feel isolated and alone. Unable to see my friends, I walked down the aisles of the local market searching for someone, anyone, to connect with. But the masks that were necessary to protect us also kept us from seeing one another.

Again, I sought out my Camino friends, curious about how the pandemic was affecting life in Brazil. In Sweden. In Germany and India. With things closed down and nowhere to go, I looked forward to hearing from them. As the pandemic dragged on, in the days and months ahead, their texts and emails became a sort of life line. In this time of isolation, they helped me feel less alone. And on those days when I felt down, I took solace in knowing there was someone out there going through the same thing.

And drag on it did. To stay grounded I began to take longer walks with my dogs out a long country road near my home. As I paused to watch the grazing cattle and listen to the manic singing of the swallows in a nearby oak tree, I thought often about those days on the Camino. As I looked out on the fields of yellow mustard that dotted the green hillsides, I bathed in the warmth of the midday sun. I found that walking, like it had on the Camino, gave me a chance to slow down, to disconnect from the stress of the day and root myself in the moment.

Almost a year after I finished my Camino, I was still trying to put the fragments of my experience together. Like the disparate pieces of a puzzle, my memories drifted again and again to the people I'd met. Their faces appeared in my thoughts, my dreams and the stories I told my friends. But try as I might, as I pieced together different sections of the puzzle, the overall scene was still not clear. I struggled to make sense of it all.

One day, as I was walking my dogs, I found myself listening to the audiobook of Richard Rohr's *The Universal Christ*. The book was recommended to me by my friend Rolf. We met when he was a social work student and I was working in my first real social work job. Rolf was an unusual soul. He had three master's degrees. In Philosophy, World Religions and Social Work. He was one of the most thoughtful and thought provoking people I knew.

Rolf and I began to meet regularly to talk about religion, faith and spirituality. Ever since I'd returned home from the Camino I'd been thinking about the question of faith and of what my experiences on the Camino could teach me about my own. He was the perfect person to try to unpack the thoughts that still lingered. Sitting around a blazing fire, beneath a towering circle of redwood trees, he listened as I tried to put into words what was stirring in my heart, but it wasn't until I heard Rohr's words that it all began to make sense.

Rohr is a Christian mystic and his thoughts on spirituality were unlike anything I'd ever heard before. Rather than finite, an image of Christianity and faith that was hampered by rules and structure, I found his words expansive, as if I had been given a window into a world much bigger than I had been led to believe existed. In one chapter, Rohr says that love is the path through which we find our way to God. All human loves, passions and preoccupations can lead us there. "Whatever elicits the flow for you," he says, "In that moment and encounter, that thing is God for you... God is Relationship Itself."

I felt a chill run through my body as I repeated those words to myself. *God is Relationship Itself.*

I had long understood how important people were in my life. My relationships with family, friends and colleagues meant everything to me. They brought me joy. Gave me comfort. A sense of connection and a place where I belonged. It was in those connections that I found my identity. And yet I recognized that human relationships were not without their challenges. Like most, I'd both caused and experienced my own share of heartache and pain. Still, even in the darkest moments, there was no other place I'd rather be.

But my view of relationship was myopic. Rohr does not suggest that the Relationship he refers to is solely human. We have relationships with all sorts of things. In fact, he dedicates the book to his beloved black Lab, Venus, who passed away as he was writing the book. In his dedication he says, "Without any apology, lightweight theology, or fear of heresy, I can appropriately say, that Venus was also Christ for me." What struck me as I listened to his words was the acknowledgement that God is in the *between*, in the thing that is created when *two or more are gathered.*

And that's when I finally understood. When the pieces came together and the larger picture finally became clear. The people. The stories. The storks nesting in the bell towers and the fields of bright red poppies. The struggle to understand my faith and the connection I felt to all of it. It wasn't separate. It was all part of the same picture. Away from the distractions of daily life, I was able to be in Relationship with it all, even the things I had so often taken for granted. I hadn't had to look very hard. God was there all along.

On the Camino, something inside me had shifted. I could feel it in my bones. I left one person. I returned home another.

I could see it most clearly in my relationship with Bob. We have been married for more than 30 years. That's a long time to be with one person. For better and sometimes for worse, our lives became predictable. After all those years I was sure I knew everything there was to know about him. I knew his answers to questions even before I asked him and could predict, with 99% certainty, what I shouldn't even ask in the first place. My sense of him became my truth; my perception my reality.

But I was wrong. T.S. Elliot wrote, "And the end of all our exploring will be to arrive where we started and know the place for the first time." Bob's text messages had surprised me. They were funny and tender. Imaginative and playful. It was as if he were showing me a part of himself for the very first time. Or maybe it had been there all along.

In the year that it took to write this book, when the world was as still as it had ever been, we spent almost every minute of every day together. Like most people, we walked our dogs. We missed our loved ones and we watched a lot of television. Still, there were new things to discover. I laughed when he lovingly refilled the birdfeeder for the second time one morning. *"We can't have them going to someone else's house," he'd said.* Some days, when I returned to my office, I'd find a cartoon or recipe he'd clipped from the morning paper taped to the monitor. I smiled as he texted back and forth with my niece, teasing her about her favorite sports teams. *"Who are you and what have you done with my husband?"* I'd asked when I received one of his exchanges on the Camino. And yet the truth was, he was the same man I'd married; only now I was able to see him more clearly.

The change in me caused a trickle effect. Now that I was able to appreciate the person Bob was, it created space for him to bring more of himself to our relationship. There was a new vitality between us, a playfulness that had been missing since the early days. And although it was a difficult year for some of the couples I knew, many of whom were struggling, we thrived together in a way we hadn't in a very long time. Almost two years after I finished walking, the Camino was still working its magic.

One February evening, I stood outside and looked at the night sky. It was a clear night. The air was crisp and the sky was filled with stars. As I often did, I looked for the Big Dipper, the one constellation I always seemed to be able to recognize. There she was, circling the North Star, just beginning the slow ascent to her highest spot in the spring sky. That afternoon I received my first COVID vaccine and I was feeling hopeful. Maybe finally, we were finding our way out of the darkness.

I thought back to that day in Carrión de los Condes when I'd received the paper star after Mass in the cathedral. "This is to remind you that you are the light," the sister said to us. "Like stars in the sky, you are called to bring light into the world. One by one, you can be the light for someone. But remember that we are not alone. Each night the sky is full of stars. Like the stars in the sky, when we join together, we can illuminate even the darkest night."

At the time I'd heard the words as a reminder to be a star for someone else, to serve to illuminate the darkness that so often surrounded us all. As the pandemic raged on, I found myself making an extra effort to reach out to my students. To the people I passed on my morning walks. In the grocery store or at the post office. It seemed like we all needed a little light these days.

But now, as I looked at the stars above me, I realized that I too had been the recipient of the light of the many people I'd met as I walked along The Way. I thought about Hugh, Conor and Emma. About Oklahoma, Patrick and Maria. I thought about all those conversations with Debbie and Pat and Irish English John and I smiled as I remembered the day I heard Marc and Martina coming up behind me, singing. About Annabella and Benny and dear, sweet Peggy. I thought about all of them and so many more. They had been my North Star, the guiding light in my journey.

I will return to the Camino one day. Of that I am sure. But as I learned while I walked, I do not know where the path will lead. I am not in control of what comes next. It is my job to stay open. To be present. To remember to be the light.

And to always keep walking.

Acknowledgements

Like walking the Camino, writing a book is a journey that is enriched and illuminated by the people who help you along the way. I am forever grateful.

To my husband Bob, whose continuous support means so much to me - Thank you for encouraging me to follow my heart and take this journey. Thank you for reading my early drafts and for all those burrito runs when I was up to my ears in revisions.

To my editor, writing coach and friend Elaine Silver - Thank you for your wisdom, your clarity and your constant guidance. Thank you for making me a better writer.

To Amy Wilkerson-Dazzo - Thank you for bringing my words to life with your beautiful illustrations. They are so much more than I could have ever imagined.

To Lesley McCullaugh, Gina Pierucci and Maura Thurman - Thank you for reading my early drafts and sharing your honest and valuable feedback.

To fellow pilgrims Mark Krahling and Hannah Bartee – Thank you for sharing your own experiences walking the Camino and answering my hundreds of questions.

To Stevan Nikolic and Adelaide Books, New York - Thank you for partnering with me, once again, to bring my story into the world.

And last, but perhaps most importantly, to all the people I met along the Camino, some of whose stories are included in this book. It is through moments spent together that this 779 kilometer walk turned into a journey I will never forget. Despite the miles between us, I carry you with me in my heart. Thank you all, for sharing your light with me.

About the Author

Suzanne Maggio is an award winning author of The Cardinal Club - A Daughter's Journey to Acceptance. A licensed clinical social worker, Maggio has helped hundreds of families improve their relationships by encouraging them to open their hearts and share their stories. She now trains the new generation of helpers as a university lecturer in Psychology, Counseling and Social Work.

Maggio is the granddaughter of Italian immigrants, a passionate cook, frequent traveler and avid baseball fan. She attended her first New York Mets baseball game at the age of eight with her grandfather, a former sports writer from Italy.

Estrellas, Moments of Illumination Along El Camino de Santiago is her second book. Her debut memoir, The Cardinal Club - A Daughter's Journey to Acceptance is published by Adelaide Books, New York and was a finalist in the 2021 Next Generation Indie Book Awards and the 2020 Independent Book Awards. In 2016 she earned a silver award from Travelers Tales for "Yo Soy," a story about the search for identity while traveling in Nicaragua.

She lives in Northern California with her husband, where they raised their two sons and where they now manage two rambunctious dogs and a brood of demanding chickens.

Made in the USA
Las Vegas, NV
02 March 2022

44916610R00127